Don't Worry about Socrates

Books by Josef Pieper from St. Augustine's Press

Don't Worry about Socrates

Josef Pieper

ST. AUGUSTINE'S PRESS

South Bend, Indiana

Manufactured in the United States of America.

1 2 3 4 5 6   23 22 21 20 19 18

Library of Congress Cataloging in Publication Data
Names: Pieper, Josef, 1904-1997, author.
Farrelly, Daniel J., 1934-, translator.
Title: "Don't Worry about Socrates", Three plays for television
Josef Pieper; translation by Dan Farrelly.
Description: South Bend, Indiana: St. Augustine's Press, 2016.
Originally published under title:
Khummert euch nicht um Sokrates.
Identifiers: LCCN 2016012551
ISBN 9781587311956 (clothbound: alk. paper)
ISBN 9781587311963 (paperbound: alk. paper)
Subjects: LCSH: Socrates--Drama.
Pieper, Josef, 1904-1997--Translations into English.
Classification: LCC PT2631.I38 A2 2016
DDC 832/.914--dc23 LC
record available at https://lccn.loc.gov/2016012551

¥ The paper used in this publication meets the minimum require-
ments of the American National Standard for Information Sciences -
Permanence of Paper for Printed Materials, ANSI Z39.48-1984.

St. Augustine's Press
www.staugustine.net

GORGIAS
OR: THE ABUSE OF WORDS AND POWER

For Dr. Clemens Münster on the occasion of his 60th birthday.

Characters

SOCRATES

GORGIAS

POLOS

CALLICLES

YOUNG WOMAN

SPEAKER

PROFESSOR

WRITER

JOURNALIST

POLITICIAN

Because Plato's "Gorgias" dialogue is framed within a modern dialogue, each actor, with one exception, has two roles to play. Both roles are connected, insofar as the characters of the frame dialogue are intimately related to and connected with those of the Platonic dialogue – something which, however, should not be made too directly obvious.

CHARACTERS

The PROFESSOR *is an expert in and lover of ancient philosophy. He does not come across as professorial. He is a likeable man, and serious. There is no academic ceremony about him. He is realistic and single-minded. His superiority is tempered and made bearable by his good-natured self-irony. He is about sixty years old. – He has to be able to switch, imperceptibly, so to speak, and with credibility, into the role of Socrates. It must be said about this latter figure that precisely the Socrates of the Platonic dialogue "Gorgias" combines characteristics which don't easily fit together and which Plato otherwise distributes between several dialogues: thought which is accurate to the point of pedantry, a serious sense of responsibility, and pathos; on the other hand, a love of irony amounting almost to sarcasm, a love of parody and caricature, and playful delight in dialectical tricks.*

The WRITER, *a fairly well-known author, is about the same age as the Professor and is a friend of his. In his attitude he combines a somewhat uneasy self-assuredness, based on his intelligence and public success, with a lack of metaphysical soundness which his friendly scepticism partly admits and partly covers up. – The Platonic* GORGIAS *is an unusual literary talent who understands the magic of language. Spoilt by his public success he is not ready for the kind of criticism which Socrates has in store* for him. He is, despite all his traditionally and socially dictated "decency," fundamentally a nihilist.

The JOURNALIST, *clearly a representative of the "young generation," is a restless spirit; quickly inflamed, choleric, with a tendency to fanaticism; witty, experienced, critical – sometimes to the point of being tactless. – POLOS is a disciple and "assistant" of Gorgias. On the one hand, he is committed to the master's teaching, of which he is an ardent advocate; on the other hand, he is more consistent and radical than Gorgias in his utter detachment.*

The POLITICIAN *knows the Professor and the writer from their student days, but he is younger than both. The writer is staying with him as a guest for a few days. He is an educated manager type; completely taken up with his directly practical and political responsibilities, he shows his respect for the literary and intellectual themes. He has no spontaneous interest in them, but his attitude is polite and correct. Occasionally he stresses the "realistic" aspect of his own point of view. – The CALLICLES of the Platonic dialogue is not, like Gorgias and Polos, an "intellectual," but a practical man of politics. He embodies the man who is not at all concerned with truth. For him, the study of reality and the achieving of objectives are two completely separate spheres: the "search for truth," belonging to the "green table" category, is a hindrance to the person who wants to make something happen in the practical sphere.*

The YOUNG WOMAN *is a companion of the Journalist. They are friends, but she is fundamentally different from him as a person and in her attitude. She is the only character who has no role to play in the Platonic dialogue. She is intellectually bright, but her calmness gives her a superior air. She is friendly and, from a distance, respectful to the Professor; she is devoted to him without knowing him very well. Through her single-minded, common-sense questioning which is aimed at accuracy and concreteness, she strives for clarification of the Platonic text, which the audience also needs.*

SCENE OF THE ACTION

The Professor's spacious study. In gaps in the bookshelves are enlarged photos of Classical Greek landscapes as well as statues of ancient philosophers, among them the Socrates figure by Lysippus [from London] and the Plato bust [from the Vatican]. Adjoining the study there is an ante-room through which the guests are led in.

Fade into an 18th century depiction of the Acropolis. The frame of the picture is not visible. This is followed by the title and the credits. – As the camera slowly pulls back and brings a part of the study into view, the speaker, remaining invisible, begins:

SPEAKER: The following debate begins here and today in the present time. And it constantly returns to it. But for the most part, and more importantly, it plays in the Athens of the great Classical period from the turn of the fifth to the fourth century BC. The author of this ancient conversation also lived more than two thousand years ago: he is Plato, one of the ancestors of all European philosophizing down to the present day. Precisely this, amongst other things, is evidence of his greatness: the passing of the millennia has had hardly any effect on the freshness of his words and the weight of his arguments. And the very concretely drawn figures which Plato, in his dialogues, brings together in conversation with one another and with the incomparable one, Socrates – philosopher, stone mason, and witness to truth, condemned by the Athenians to death by poisoning with hemlock in 399 BC. These human characters, too, are with us today just as they were in those days: the man of unquestioning commitment to the practical exercise of political power; the nihilistic wordsmith exposed to any influence that promises profit; and also the one who, like Socrates, unwavering in his quest for truth and justice, he too – as is urgently to be hoped – can be found in our age no less than at any other time.

Herewith the characters in our play, at least the most important of them, have been named.

Now the Professor can be seen, laying out glasses, bottles, and cigarettes.

As I said, it starts here and today in the study of a University lecturer. It is a summer evening, about ten o'clock. More guests are expected; one of them, especially, is a famous writer whose name everyone knows; he is a friend of the host since their student days.

The Professor looks at his watch.

He has just finished his public lecture, probably a few minutes ago, and must already be on his way here.

The Professor switches on the two standard lamps and the desk lamp.

Hopefully the spoilt and ambitious man can be convinced that it was not possible, on this occasion, to be there to "sit at his feet."

The doorbell rings

The Professor goes out to let in the arriving guests. Voices can be heard outside.

WRITER: ... But it is not worth mentioning – please ...

PROFESSOR: No, it is ...

In the meantime, the politician enters first. His eye roves over the bookshelves with respectful interest. A moment later the host leads the writer into the study.

WRITER *laughing*: I would never have gone there myself – certainly not after the way it was announced.

PROFESSOR: So you only go to your own lectures? *Is about to collect a drink but turns back again.* Yes, the announcement. It wasn't very clear. What was it, then – a reading from your books? Or did you give a lecture?

POLITICIAN *before the Writer can answer*: Both! It was both. And both were magnificent. The audience, the room – there wasn't an empty seat – people were very enthusiastic. I watched them intently. You really missed something. Only one thing was terrible – *with some ceremony he takes out a cigar case, laughing* – I was starving the whole time. Is it permitted here?

PROFESSOR *producing a box of cigars*: But, of course – or are you particular? Oh, yes, I see you are! Something exquisite?

The politician has already taken a cigar from his own case and is handling it appreciatively; during what follows he is completely preoccupied with the ritual of lighting a cigar.

POLITICIAN: Would you mind if I were to stay with this one ...?

PROFESSOR: Not at all.

The Writer waits, smiling patiently; he is visibly somewhat weary but also animated by his success; he speaks about it a little too casually.

WRITER: Yes, first I said a few fundamental things. The structural changes in modern literature, in general. And then I read. Most of it not yet published. "Not yet" published – perhaps it never will be; perhaps it will never be "finished" …

PROFESSOR *interrupting him*: That would be bad! All the more so since I wasn't there … *He hesitates for a short while and then continues in a different, more serious tone*: No! You know, it's good for a change that we have no cause to argue. Do you not agree? We are nearly always on the point of quarrelling. Do you remember?

WRITER *who clearly wants to avoid a serious, objective discussion*:
Quarrel? No! We have discussed, debated, argued, if you like. I always found it very entertaining …

PROFESSOR: Tell me, anyway: what are they talking about these days.=? I live out in the provinces, you know. *He points to the bookshelves.* My daughter – you saw her the last time; in the meantime, she has become a wild admirer of your books; I am to give you her greetings and to tell you she is very sad, disappointed, inconsolable – and so on and so forth; well, this daughter of mine finds one particular essay of yours especially important; naturally, she doesn't say "important;" she says "fantastic," "heavenly" – the essay about artificiality. Have you written on that subject recently?

WRITER *emphasising the exact wording, as one who is quoting:* Yes! "Against condemnation of the artificial." I have written about that recently. But it was published only a few days ago. All praise to your daughter that she knows about it already and even seems to have read it. And she finds it "heavenly" into the bargain!

PROFESSOR: So, that's the latest! Breaking a lance for the artificial! But what do you mean by it?
The writer seems about to give a detailed answer but then is clearly not in the mood for a serious and strenuous explanation.

WRITER: What I mean is the following: the difference between the natural and the artificial is wildly exaggerated. There is not really an essential difference. Basically, there isn't one. The artificial is everything that man makes, produces. Cars, refrigerators, physical and philosophical theories, poems – all of that is just as "natural" as what we find existing in the world around us, as "nature," man himself included …

PROFESSOR: But you are not being serious?! The thing is …
The doorbell rings.
The Professor is somewhat concerned. He is slightly annoyed. He stands up and turns to go to the ante-room.
What? More visitors? Now? One moment. I have no help today.

WRITER *suddenly remembering:* Oh, that has to be Dr Rudolf. With his colleague. I had almost forgotten. You don't mind?

PROFESSOR *at first not seeming particularly pleased*: Dr Rudolf? That's the journalist? Yes, I know him. His writing is sometimes quite witty. Especially when he's "against" something.

WRITER: Exactly. That is his strength. Or also his weakness – whichever way you look at it. Sometimes he is a bit difficult to deal with. It is all to the good that this young lady is accompanying him. There seems to be some kind of tie between them. She is also a "Doctor," a Doctor of Law, I think.

POLITICIAN: No, a Doctor of Political Science. She writes mainly about social politics.
The bell rings again. Professor goes off with a gesture that speaks volumes. The politician is enjoying his cigar. He looks around the room and points to the books
A real hide-away, eh? A wonderful hermitage! Sometimes I dream of such a thing – believe it or not.

WRITER *laughs*: Well, I don't believe it. Dream – perhaps. But you couldn't survive one day living here.
The Professor enters with the two new guests.

PROFESSOR *turning to the young woman*: No! No! Not in the least. I'm delighted. You know one another already?

JOURNALIST: We were together only ten minutes ago.
Brief greetings through gestures and smiles, etc.

YOUNG WOMAN *relaxed, looking discreetly around the room; then without any trace of effusiveness, but more taking note*: So this is where you live!

PROFESSOR *laughs*: Yes, this is where I work.

YOUNG WOMAN: In complete isolation …

PROFESSOR: I'll have to disappoint you again: I also sometimes invite my students to come here. This summer, for example, we will be reading Plato together here.

YOUNG WOMAN: So – a kind of symposium?

PROFESSOR: Yes, if you like. In a circle of between eight and ten people.
The following conversation takes place while the Professor passes around glasses, pours drinks, offers cigarettes.

WRITER: In Greek?

PROFESSOR: No, not in Greek. Unfortunately, we can't require that anymore. But I don't find that as bad as some of my colleagues do. I am basically less concerned with the language than with the substance.

WRITER: But a really good English translation is hardly available.

PROFESSOR: That is perhaps a slight exaggeration. But, in fact, for these Plato readings I do the translations myself.

POLITICIAN: That's something I would love to be able to do: to read Plato, completely cut off from the world, far away from all politics …

YOUNG WOMAN *with good-natured irony*: You, "far away from all politics" – I'd like to see that!

WRITER *laughing*: That is the kind of self-deception that only befalls the extremely practical man.

YOUNG WOMAN: But it doesn't befall them at all. They only act as though it did.
The journalist inspects the bookshelves uninhibitedly and takes down individual volumes.

JOURNALIST: Browsing is not forbidden?

PROFESSOR: No! Educate yourself to your heart's

content! *To the Politician:* By the way, Plato is not as far away from all politics as you might think. The students, anyway, are continually surprised that we are always being confronted with actuality. Precisely in "Gorgias!" *To the Young Woman:* That is the dialogue we are reading at present. Unexpectedly we are speaking about things which worry us just as much today as they did Socrates and Plato in those days.

YOUNG WOMAN: Do you really mean that Plato speaks about things that concern us today? What notion could they have had, two thousand years ago, about our problems, the problems of the atomic age? I would really find …

POLITICIAN *who has for a long time been contemplating the portrait of Socrates:* Excuse me – who is that?

PROFESSOR *who was about to answer the Young Woman:* Whom do you mean?

POLITICIAN *points with his cigar at the Socrates image:* I mean the faun here.

JOURNALIST *in a low voice, looking at the ceiling:* Oh, oh, oh! And that in this house!

WRITER *with the deliberate casualness of the connoisseur:* That is the London Socrates – by Lysippus – isn't it?

PROFESSOR *not answering the Journalist and the Writer:* Yes, that is Socrates. But "faun" – not bad! His friends referred to him as a Silenus. A figure that could be opened up and "inside a divine image" – said Alcibiades in the Symposium, when he was already a bit drunk. Besides, there is another story about this, related by Cicero.

The Young Woman has gone up to the bust of Socrates and now swings around.

YOUNG WOMAN: Please tell us. There seems to be a special point to it. Or am I wrong?

PROFESSOR: Correct! A very unexpected point, too. So – one day a famous physiognomist comes to Athens. In the market place he joins the circle of people around Socrates, whom he has never seen before. This man wants to show what he can do and begins to interpret his character from this faun-like face. You can imagine the result: desire for pleasure, sensuousness, disorderliness – only bad things.

WRITER *very interested*: Oh, I didn't know that story. Or I had forgotten it.

PROFESSOR: Yes, but now here it comes! The circle around Socrates had listened – taken aback, silent – and then there were peals of laughter. Only one person did not laugh: Socrates himself. He said: this man is completely right; that's what I would have become if Logos had not saved me from it.

YOUNG WOMAN *who has listened with visibly growing interest*: Logos? You mean reason?

PROFESSOR *hesitantly*: Reason – that doesn't quite express the full sense, although it is part of it. Truth would be closer, but …
The Journalist, in his browsing, has arrived at the host's writing table and at the printouts of Gorgias texts which he is already paging through.

JOURNALIST: I beg your pardon. I presume this is the text that you are at present reading with your students? And the translation is yours?

PROFESSOR: Yes, the translation – and above all the abridging of it. As I said, the things of purely historical interest in Plato don't occupy me much. What fascinates me is what is still relevant to us today. And that is really quite a lot.

YOUNG WOMAN: I wanted to ask you earlier: in what way is this particular dialogue relevant today?

The Young Woman asks the Journalist, who has joined the others again, for one of the stapled copies of the text he has in his hands. In a low voice she reads the title: Plato's "Gorgias." So who was that then?

PROFESSOR: That's a long story. – If I had to give the dialogue a title I would call it: "Politics and Oratory."

YOUNG WOMAN: "Oratory"?

JOURNALIST: A hopelessly ancient business. Completely passé.

PROFESSOR: On the contrary! Very much part of the present day! Of course the word "oratory" is antiquated. Nobody today speaks of oratory. But the substance, what is meant …

YOUNG WOMAN *interrupting*: And what is meant?

PROFESSOR: The meaning is – well, "journalism!" *To the Journalist:* Your very own trade. Journalism, writing, literature, radio commentary – all kinds of things. Public word-usage in general. Of course, carried out methodically and with an understanding of art. Something like that.

YOUNG WOMAN *paging through the text, then, as if trying out the word, she says very quickly:* "Word-usage," "word-usage;" good, "politics and public usage of words!" I must say that certainly sounds very up-to-date. And does Plato have a definite – theory – about this?

PROFESSOR *hesitantly*: "Theory" – the word we use today has a different meaning for Plato …

WRITER *interrupting*: But these dialogues are above all poetic structures. We could say they are dramatic works in prose. In any case, we are dealing with shaping a text and not with "theory," and not with propositions. All that is something completely different.

PROFESSOR *pensively*: Stop a moment! That does not have to be something "completely different!" As you very well know. You say "shaping," but not "statement." I would say that in the case of Plato and his dialogues it is a question of statement through literary shaping. Certainly there are theses, "theory," even political theory …

POLITICIAN *who has now been listening with rapt attention, interrupts spontaneously*: "Political theory" – there is no such thing! "Theory" is one thing and "politics" is another thing – a totally un-theoretical thing! Here we are simply dealing with the exercise of power!

YOUNG WOMAN *interrupting*: Oh, and possibly a few other things as well!!

POLITICIAN: No, dear lady, we are dealing purely with the conflict between power blocks. With the assertion of one's own interests, without any theory. *Turning to the Writer*: And so here we are in agreement, it would seem: we shouldn't mix up things which have nothing to do with one another. For me, what is wonderful about things like philosophy, poetry, and also about Plato is that they have nothing – but absolutely nothing – to do with politics, which since time began was always a very robust business in which one easily gets the famously "dirty hands." It is marvellous that one can keep on turning one's back on these things. We can enter a completely different world, lock the door behind us and find ourselves, for example, in this academic hideaway. We read Plato and we forget politics. And now suddenly all of this here *he indicates the surrounding array of books and images* is to be politicized? That's awful!

WRITER *turning to the Politician*: Yes, indeed, we are in agreement. Who would have thought it! But I would say, almost in agreement. After all, politics is not merely blind praxis. You will grant me that. There is also politically engaged literature. Literature is not simply there. It has an effect, and a political one at that. But – you are quite right, alongside it there is, thank God, also the quite different thing, *poésie pure*, pure form, pure thought …

PROFESSOR *interrupting*: What is meant by "pure" in this context? "Pure" of what?

WRITER *after brief reflection*: "Pure" – of all commitment to ends! Independent! Also independent of all norms – except, of course, of the law of form itself. "Pure form," pure thought" – that also amounts to freedom, I would say. Freedom from everything – perhaps even from all reality. Here I am referring to the philistine's stuffy reality of the trivial and banal, and so on.

}15{

Yes, and this independence, freedom, this "purity" – this is the essential element in literature, and also in true philosophy, I would say. Surely this is also what is great in Plato. Or do you not agree?

PROFESSOR *laughs*: Quite simply: No! But that is yet again an inadmissible simplification.

YOUNG WOMAN *interrupts*: Simplifications are never harmful, in my opinion. Unacceptable complications are much worse!

PROFESSOR *turning to the others*: That is true! But do you know what makes me laugh?

JOURNALIST: Probably that this – I am quoting – "scholar's hideaway" has inspired a practical politician to make a philosophical speech …

PROFESSOR: No. What amuses me is that we have landed right in the middle of Plato's "Gorgias." It's a pity that my students can't hear us. *He turns to the Young Woman, who is still nursing the open Gorgias text on her knees. He, too, now picks up a copy of the text.* That is exactly what is being dealt with here.

YOUNG WOMAN: Excuse me, Professor. How do you mean "exactly"? What, exactly, is being dealt with? Politics?

PROFESSOR: Yes, that too. But what I have in mind mainly is "pure thought!" It is a question of the supposedly "pure" literature which is assumed to be concerned with pure "form," perfect form, a work of art in words, which, however, by the same token [because it is, in principle, indifferent towards all content] can serve any particular ends – above all, political ones, the interests of power – and does, in fact, let itself be used in this way.

YOUNG WOMAN: I find that absolutely fascinating. So that's the way we'd have to see Plato interpreted! – But you also wanted to tell me what kind of character this Gorgias is …

PROFESSOR: He is, in brief, the representative of "pure" literature, literature that is taken to be pure.

YOUNG WOMAN: And he gets into conversation with Socrates? The sparks must be flying there!

PROFESSOR: Yes, it's murderous. – But there are some other characters as well, more dangerous than Gorgias. The most important one is Callicles, a orator …

YOUNG WOMAN *interrupts*: And so also a – "journalist"?

PROFESSOR: No. No. "Orator" in ancient terminology is something different again …

JOURNALIST: "Oratory" does mean "journalism," but the orator is not a journalist! Very enlightening!

YOUNG WOMAN *jokingly reproving the Journalist*: Rodolfo! Please let him finish! *To the Professor:* So Callicles is not a colleague of Gorgias?

PROFESSOR: No! No more than a parliamentarian is the same as a skilled speaker.

POLITICIAN *laughing loudly*: But there is such a thing!

PROFESSOR *turning to the Politician*: Of course, "parliamentarian," from "parlare," literally does mean "speaker." But the essential thing for a politician is not literature but political praxis. Agreed?

YOUNG WOMAN: Of course, agreed!

PROFESSOR: Now Gorgias is an intellectual, a literary man, a professor of oratory; but Callicles, the orator, is a political practitioner!

YOUNG WOMAN *examining the text*: There is another name here: Polos or P los? *She pronounces the name, trying out first the short and then the long 'o' sound.*

PROFESSOR: Yes, P los – that is a young, somewhat forward intellectual …

YOUNG WOMAN *to the Journalist*: Rodolfo, did you hear that? That's you: "a young forward intellectual!"

JOURNALIST *with an ironic gesture of acceptance*: Who, of course, is put in his place – I suspect by Socrates.

PROFESSOR: Yes, that kind of thing.

YOUNG WOMAN *with visibly growing interest*: And you read that with your students, playing different roles?

PROFESSOR: Yes, naturally, each playing a role. The students really enjoy that.

YOUNG WOMAN: Would it be possible to join in some time?
The Professor at first shows friendly dissent, but then seems to be wondering.

WRITER *paging through the text, stopping to read here and there*: That thing about poésie pure I find naturally very interesting. This Gorgias …

POLITICIAN *half laughing, half with annoyance and ironic resignation*: OK, then get started!

PROFESSOR: We've started already, a long way back. We already in the middle of it!

POLITICIAN: All right, I'm listening. *Looking at his cigar:* It will be a pleasure to listen.

PROFESSOR: Your cue does not come until the last act in any case. Perhaps you can think about it in the meantime.
The Politician makes lame signs that he is opting out.
Of course, I enjoy this. – Where do we begin?

YOUNG WOMAN: Is there a role for me as well? Or are women not allowed access to the symposium?

PROFESSOR: In Plato's Symposium a woman is even the main character: Diotima. Of course, she is not physically present. And here in Gorgias, as you quite rightly suspect, there are no women at all. But I think there is a role for you, and a very important one: you are the supervisor!

YOUNG WOMAN *laughing*: But what am I to supervise?

PROFESSOR: That we, the male intellect, don't lose sight of reality!

YOUNG WOMAN: And how am I to do that? I can't wait!

PROFESSOR: For example, by protesting! By asking the shockingly concrete and simple questions. As soon as you feel that the discussion is getting lost in abstractions you simply ask for clarification: "Excuse me, what does that mean exactly, in concrete terms?"

YOUNG WOMAN: I'm surely not meant to correct Plato.

PROFESSOR: Well, perhaps not Plato – but, for example, my translation. I'm not yet entirely happy with it.

Besides, we won't be limiting ourselves for very long to a patient reading of Plato ...

YOUNG WOMAN: So, I'm to ask the dumb questions? Not a very rewarding role!

PROFESSOR: Don't say anything against "dumb questions." They are the only questions which Socrates thought were worth bothering about. – So, where do we begin? *The Professor pages back and forth through the book first quickly and then slowly.*

At the beginning it looks like this: Socrates comes to the house of Callicles, the politician. Gorgias, who has stopped off there, had just finished a lecture, a festive lecture, with enormous success. Socrates arrives late. "That's the way to do it when there is war," Callicles calls out to him, "turn up when everything is over."

Callicles, you see, has just emerged from the house with his famous guest. *In a somewhat different tone, pondering:* And by the way, this idea the director, Plato, has of showing the literary and the political star arm in arm seems to me some kind of statement. "A statement through form!"

POLITICIAN: What could – sorry, I find this interesting – what could this statement be?

PROFESSOR: About how much political success and the oratory of the sophist are ... can be ...linked!

So: Socrates asks if he may pose this famous traveler a question, something very simple. Basically, it is only one single question: namely, what is, precisely, this activity – carried out like a profession – this business of "oratory"?

JOURNALIST: In other words, journalism!

YOUNG WOMAN: Rodolfo!
Laughter.

PROFESSOR: Yes, but I think there is nothing we can do
except let this old word stand.
In any case, in those days – at the time of Socrates –
the word "oratory" seems to have been something
super-modern. When, therefore, Gorgias says,"My
business is oratory," you have to realize that above all
he is laying claim to avant-garde modernity. There is
no completely accurate word for "oratory" in our language any more;just as there is none for "gymnast,"
which we'll talk about shortly. Therefore, let's simply
talk about "oratory" and "gymnast" – I don't find that
so bad. – All right, Socrates then says – *he turns to the
Young Woman* – have you found the passage? At the
top of page four; yes, that's it. *Turning to the Writer:*
And you take the part of Gorgias?
*The Writer, who has just drunk some of his wine, nods vig-
orously.*
Excellent!

SOCRATES: Fine, my dear Gorgias, you claim you understand oratory and that you can coach others in it. Then
what is oratory about? What does it relate to?

GORGIAS: To the way we handle words.

SOCRATES: What words? What sort of words? There are
words which, let's say, are meant to make clear to the
sick what they need to do in order to become well
again …

GORGIAS: Naturally, I don't mean words of that kind.

SOCRATES: Therefore oratory is not concerned with just any kind of words?

GORGIAS: No. That's quite obvious.

SOCRATES: But it makes one capable of dealing with words.

GORGIAS: Yes, but where the words are, at the same time, the decisive factor.

SOCRATES: Good. There are activities which, like painting or sculpture, take place in complete silence. And there are other arts which cannot do without words and in which the whole effect depends on the use of words. And oratory is an art of this kind?

GORGIAS: Naturally!

SOCRATES: But there are also obviously arts which cannot do without words and which, however, you would not call oratory – let's say, for example, astronomy. Astronomy speaks – essentially! – about the movement of the stars and the reciprocal relationships of their speeds .... So, please tell me what, by contrast, oratory relates to. What are the things that words talk about that oratory is concerned with?

GORGIAS *after a pause, with emphasis*: They are, my dear Socrates, they are the most important and the most significant human things.

SOCRATES *at first seeming impressed, but then hesitantly and with slight irony*: That is an answer, Gorgias! But – but is suffers a little from lack of precision. It still seems to me too vague.

But you know the drinking song: The best thing is to be healthy; beauty is next; and then: to become rich through honest means ... ?

GORGIAS *hastily*: I know the song, but how is it relevant here?

SOCRATES: Well, the masters of these three things praised will now make their plea: the doctor, the gymnast, and the money-man. The doctor will say to me: "Gorgias is deceiving you; the most important things for human beings is what my art deals with." And the gymnast will also say: "My task is to make them physically beautiful." And the businessman, the money-maker – he'll despise them all and say to me: "My dear Socrates, just think about it; can you think of anything that for Gorgias or for anyone else is more important than money?" Therefore, my dear Gorgias, you must answer not just these three people but also me: what do you consider is the most important thing, the highest good for us that you say your art is concerned with? What is it?

GORGIAS: Freedom for oneself and power over others: that is, if the truth be known, the highest good!

SOCRATES: What do you mean by that? I'd like to know exactly what you mean.

GORGIAS: I mean that one is able, through the art of speaking, to persuade people to do some particular thing. "People" ... in court that refers to the judges, in council the councillors, in a public gathering the people, and persons, everywhere decisions have to be made. If you are master of this art you have the doctor and the gymnast in your power. And the businessman will not have gathered his wealth for himself but for someone else, namely, for you – assuming you know how to use words and convince people.

SOCRATES: Now, my dear Gorgias, you have made yourself perfectly clear. Oratory is the art of persuasion! But what this persuasion really is and what it is related to – there I have my suspicions, but some things are still unclear to me. So, what does persuasion relate to? *Silence.*
Or do you think the question is unwarranted?

GORGIAS: No, not at all. As I said, I have in mind, for example, persuasion in a court of law and in other like situations. And what it specifically deals with, *he hesitates*, is what is right and what is not right.

SOCRATES: That's more or less what I thought. But … Don't be surprised if now, although the thing seems to be clear, I have a further question. – Whether one has an opinion about something or actually knows – would you say that these are two different things? Or are they the same?

GORGIAS *slightly puzzled*: No, for me they are two different things.

SOCRATES: Then perhaps we are allowed to say: there are two different types of persuasion? One which produces an opinion and another which produces knowledge?

GORGIAS: Certainly!

SOCRATES: Well, which kind of persuasion does oratory deal with? In a court case or in a large meeting the question of "right" and "not right" is being discussed. In this case, does oratory aim to have people form an opinion about something or to know something?

GORGIAS *hesitantly*: I think to form an opinion …

SOCRATES: Therefore: oratory is the art of persuasion. But it does not really teach but achieves belief! And, indeed, with regard to right and wrong! And how could a speaker be in a position to teach a great throng of people about such important issues!

GORGIAS: Impossible!

SOCRATES: Now, let us look again: what do we now really understand by "oratory"? For my part, I am still not clear what is meant by it. If, let us say, a communal administration has to decide on the choice of doctors or the choice of shipwrights, or if there is an issue about the building of walls or the setting up of ports – in these cases those who are experts in these fields will do the work and not those who are experts in oratory. Or what do you think?
Gorgias is silent.
Just suppose that your students ask you: "What will we gain from your teaching? In what things will we have a voice? – only about right and wrong? Or also in the things about which Socrates has been speaking?"
If you would try to answer these questions …

GORGIAS: Oratory takes on everything and uses it! For example, how often have I, with my brother and with other doctors, visited a sick person who could not be persuaded to take a particular medicine or to undergo a surgical operation. Now, what the doctor could not do I was able to do: by no other means than the art of speech! I will make bold to say: if one person who is an expert in healing and another who is an expert in oratory come into a city and there is a question of getting a people's assembly or any other large gathering of people to vote for one of the two, the expert in speaking will be chosen, if he wants to – whereas the doctor will not even be considered. An expert in oratory – there is simply nothing, nothing at all about which he cannot speak more convincingly than the actual expert in the field – at least to the people.

But, of course, the same applies to oratory as to other abilities: one is not allowed to abuse it!

SOCRATES *pricks up his ears at these latter words*: What you have just said – is that compatible with what you stated earlier about oratory? *A brief pause. Then starting afresh:* So you are saying: "at least to the people." That is as much as to say: to the non-expert? For the knowledgeable, the orator will hardly be more convincing than the doctor.

GORGIAS: Clearly!

SOCRATES: It follows that the person who is expert with words can make himself more believable than the doctor. But that means that for the non-expert the non-expert is more believable than the expert. That is the result – am I right?

GORGIAS: In this case – yes!

SOCRATES: But not just in this case! Oratory obviously does not need to know the subject and the facts. One needs only to command the technique of persuasion, by which the layman is given the impression that the speaker is more expert than the expert.

GORGIAS *overcoming an initial uncertainty*: But is that not a great advantage – that one only needs to possess this one art and is still not inferior to any expert?

SOCRATES: Whether one is inferior to other masters or not if one is a master of oratory as you say – we can leave that question aside for the moment. But we want to achieve clarity about whether oratory is concerned with right and wrong, with the beautiful and the ignoble, with good and evil, just as it is with health [for example] – namely, that it knows nothing about the object itself, nothing about what is really good and bad, what is beautiful and ignoble, what is right and wrong, but rather – again – in all of these things has a command of the process of persuasion whereby the non-expert is given the impression that one who is equally non-expert knows more than the expert. Or should one already be clear about these things for oneself? If someone wants to learn about oratory from you – should he bring the above knowledge with him? Tell me your answer, my dear Gorgias.

GORGIAS: Now, my dear Socrates, if he does not already possess this knowledge he will learn it from me ... *Socrates interrupts him.*

SOCRATES: Stop! That will do for now. In any case: anyone who has had his training in oratory from you will know – because this is an essential part of it – what is right and wrong! He will either know it from earlier or from your instruction?

GORGIAS *hesitant, puzzled*: Yes, certainly!

SOCRATES: But you have said it is possible to use oratory for wrong purposes, to abuse it. That surprises me. Something is not quite right here – if at the same time, by definition, a false judgment about right and wrong is meant to be impossible?!

During the last words of Socrates the Writer has ostenta-tiously closed his copy of the text and put it on the table. He shakes his head and shrugs his shoulders. As he does so, he is looking at the Professor and the others. A pause ensues.

JOURNALIST: Finished? Now the fun starts!

WRITER *to the Professor*: No. I am disappointed. In all of that there was not a word about poésie pure. Not a syllable about "pure" literature. This Gorgias fellow stands for – what shall I say – a kind of massively goal-oriented journalism.

PROFESSOR: He does that also. But he does it very much against his will. He is forced into it. By Socrates! He is compelled to let the cat out of the bag. Then it really becomes clear that the supposedly "pure" art of speaking is above all a means to an end, for exercising power. I admit that this only becomes completely clear when one is able to see the historical Gorgias; to the ancient reader of Plato he was, of course, a very well-known figure.

YOUNG WOMAN: So Gorgias is not an invention?

PROFESSOR *turning to the Young Woman*: No – Gorgias was one of the most famous men of his time. His lecture tours through the cities of Greece must have been quite a triumphal procession.

JOURNALIST: And a mighty lucrative one as well!

PROFESSOR: Yes, you are right. Socrates refers to the fact that Gorgias paid for a statue of himself – out of pure gold – for the temple in Delphi.

POLITICIAN *banging on the table*: Good heavens! That's impressive!

JOURNALIST: That he did such a thing – or that he could afford it?

POLITICIAN: Both.

YOUNG WOMAN: I believe you!
But tell me, what was the subject of these so fantastically well-paid lectures?

PROFESSOR: Well – the fascination didn't derive from the content, anyway.

POLITICIAN: From what, then?

JOURNALIST: From the staging!

PROFESSOR: I would say: from the form, from the music of the words, from the rhythm! This magic, this almost more musical than verbal magic must have bewitched the audience – which was, by the way, the most sophisticated audience in the world at that time.

WRITER: And for that very reason it cannot have been pure trickery. We have to think of the historical Gorgias as an enormous talent.

PROFESSOR: Exactly. His impact can be clearly seen from his language. Attic Greek, through him, simply evolved. It became smoother, had more differentiation ...

WRITER *interrupting*: That should not be underestimated!

PROFESSOR: Quite right. But whatever about differentiation and verbal magic: if we consider how Plato speaks about Gorgias, in the Symposium, for example, how bitterly he makes a laugh of him – then something quite different stands out as important. Namely, the blatant lack of substance despite all his formal expertise. This man is a radical nihilist – and in such a literal sense that one can scarcely think it possible. One of his writings begins with the sentence: "There is nothing" – there is, according to this, nothing that makes it worth ...

YOUNG WOMAN: There you are! That is Jean Paul Sartre!

PROFESSOR: Right!

WRITER *slapping his hand on the text*: But that is not what we are talking about here!

PROFESSOR: True, true. But it does color what is in fact there word for word. The reader whom Plato was addressing, his contemporary, would have taken in all of that. For him it must have been exciting the way this Gorgias, this "great man," this best-selling author, was called to account by Socrates.

JOURNALIST *interrupting*: Called to account? How?

PROFESSOR: By his being forced, in the most charming and irresistible way, to take off his mask and declare openly and audibly: the entire art based on words, this littérature pure which is seemingly an end in itself, is in truth very drastically a means to other ends – in such a way that right and wrong are fundamentally a matter of indifference. – But Gorgias does shy away from expressly admitting this ultimate conclusion. *Turning to the writer and pointing to the text:* Did you notice, by the way, that you stopped right at the point at which your part, the Gorgias part, concludes?

WRITER: No, I didn't notice that. The discussion was still in full swing!
The Journalist opens the text and looks for the passage.

PROFESSOR: Yes, it was. But Gorgias falls silent. He hasn't given his answer. He would now either have to correct his original thesis or think it through to its logical conclusion. But he doesn't manage to do either.

YOUNG WOMAN: One moment, please. I didn't quite understand that. What should Gorgias now have said?

PROFESSOR: His initial thesis was as follows: oratory, the highly developed art of dealing with words, is simply geared to the gaining of power. *Turning to the Young Woman:* That, too, by the way, can be found in Sartre in a very similar formulation! Language as such is nothing but a means of exercising power.
That it belongs to the nature of human speech also to deal with things and with facts is simply suppressed. The only thing that the journalist needs to know something about, according to Gorgias, is: right and wrong. But how – and this is now Socrates! – how is one to know what is right and what is wrong if the truth of things is of no interest to him? It is very likely that for him right and wrong are just as much a matter of indifference.

YOUNG WOMAN: Superb! And that is the question Gorgias doesn't answer. That is clear.

PROFESSOR: He could very well answer, but he won't risk it – in a nice way, I would say. He could admit that talk, his own talk about right and wrong, is in fact not meant very seriously …

JOURNALIST *interrupting*: How do you find it "nice" that Gorgias does not have the courage to answer? It is, after all, the one logical thing he could have said! Feebleness of thought does not seem to me to be any sort of recommendation.

PROFESSOR: Well … I, too, would see it as a weakness. But, I can't help it, I don't find it so uncongenial; I would say it is a happy inconsistency. If the logical alternative were to be cynicism then it is perhaps not so bad to hesitate about being consistent.

YOUNG WOMAN: You said Gorgias could have done two things: either think his thesis radically through to its logical conclusions – and that was something he could not or did not want to do. And the second possibility? What else could he or should he have done?

PROFESSOR: Simply correct his thesis! Admit that language is not merely an instrument of power. That speaking does not necessarily have to be "persuasion!"

YOUNG WOMAN: And that is the last thing he can do. Yes, that is clear to me now.

PROFESSOR: This is where Gorgias suddenly stops. He hasn't finished – but he falls silent. And now Polos springs into the breach. *Turning to the Journalist:* The next generation is more consistent; traditional inhibitions are no longer of any importance. *He takes up the text again and flicks through the pages.* Polos immediately goes at Socrates aggressively: that is no way to act, it is unfair to push the other person to declare his personal position. Socrates's response is ironically to pretend he is intimidated: that's what young people are for – to point out old people's errors to them. He, Socrates, is therefore prepared to be corrected – of course, under one condition: namely, that Polos agree to a real conversation and not make long speeches.

At this point the Journalist, to everyone's amusement, abruptly takes over the role of Polos and immediately begins in a rather sharp tone.

POLOS: What? I won't be free to speak as much as I want?

SOCRATES: It would be very hard, my good man, if you had come to Athens, the city where there is complete freedom of speech, and it should be denied especially to you! But think of the other side of the coin: if you want to talk a lot and don't want to answer questions – then would it not be bad for me if I didn't have the freedom simply to go away? – So, do as Gorgias and I did: refute me and let yourself be refuted. You can choose: do you want to ask questions or do you want to answer?

POLOS: All right then, Socrates, I will ask questions and you will answer me. If Gorgias, as you say, had no clear opinion about the nature of oratory – what is your view?

SOCRATES: Do you mean, what sort of art I think it is?

POLOS: Yes.

SOCRATES: To tell you the truth, I don't think it is an art at all.

POLOS: Then what is it?

SOCRATES: Something that was discovered merely by trial and error.

POLOS: Trial and error? What was being tried?

SOCRATES: The way one produces a certain feeling of well-being, a certain kind of pleasure.

POLOS: And so at least you see oratory as a beautiful and good thing – since you are speaking of pleasure? Clearly, oratory pleases people?

SOCRATES: Well! Whether I think it is something good – that'll come later. But since you obviously put such a high value on what is pleasing: would you do something to please me?

POLOS: What would that be?

SOCRATES: Ask me what sort of art I think cooking is, the preparation of delicacies.

POLOS *unwilling*: All right – what sort of art is the art of cooking?

SOCRATES: It is not an art at all!

POLOS: Then what is it? Tell us.

SOCRATES: Something found out by experimentation.

POLOS *impatiently*: And what was the experiment?

SOCRATES: But Polos, it is obvious: the way a person produces a certain feeling of well-being, a particular pleasure!

POLOS: But the art of cooking and oratory are not the same!

SOCRATES: Of course not! But both are a piece of the same whole.

POLOS *annoyed*: What sort of whole is that?

SOCRATES: Well, if it is now not unfair to speak the truth! I am a bit worried to speak bluntly. Gorgias could perhaps think I wanted to pour scorn on his art – although I still don't know what he himself thinks it is. – Anyway, what I understand by oratory belongs to something that is not at all beautiful! A certain level of cheek is required and it is also necessary to know how to deal with people and where to hook in.
But, to talk plainly: I call it flattery. – And that comes in many different forms. One of them is oratory. But now, if you want to know what particular form I mean – you will have to ask me!

POLOS *insolently*: OK, I'm asking: what particular form of "flattery" is oratory supposed to be?

SOCRATES: Listen carefully. I consider oratory *in the tone of a quiz question* a lying imitation of a part of the art of politics.

POLOS *angrily exploding*: Now I don't understand a word you are saying!

SOCRATES *calm and provocative*: Not surprising, for I have not yet reached the point of explaining myself.
There are people who seem to feel physically well, whereas in reality they are sick; and no one notices it, except perhaps a doctor or a gymnast?

POLOS: Yes, of course, that happens.

SOCRATES: Then isn't there something that produces in

the soul the semblance of well-being – whereas the reality is quite different?

POLOS: Correct, of course.

SOCRATES: Next. There are arts which concern themselves with the true well-being – of body and soul – the art of healing and gymnastics, for example, and, in the political sphere, law-giving or also the administration of justice. These true arts, each of them, are invaded by flattery and are replaced by its lies. The good done by these arts is not in the least related to flattery. It uses the lack of judgment in people to seduce them by giving them what is most to their liking. In the art of healing, for example, the art (or pseudo art) of cooking creeps in, offering sweet things. And if a doctor, together with the creator of such delicacies, were to appear before children – and men who are as unaware as children –and have a competition about which of them knew the most about the benefit or harm of such food – the doctor would lose.
So that's what I mean by flattery! And I maintain that it is something bad because it is after what is merely pleasant and not after what really does good.

POLOS: So, in your opinion oratory is flattery ...

SOCRATES *interrupts him in a good-natured but ironical tone*: A part of it, I said. Still so young, Polos, and already such a bad memory! What will it be like later!

POLOS *who does not want to be interrupted, now speaking with the volume and tone of a demagogue*: So you are saying: our outstanding orators are flatterers and their importance for the state is zero?

SOCRATES: Is that a question you are asking me or is it the beginning of a speech?

POLOS: It is a question!

SOCRATES: Good. To my mind they have no importance.

POLOS: No importance! And yet they are the most powerful people in the state – or is that not so?

SOCRATES: No! Unless by power you mean something that is good for the person who has it.

POLOS: Yes, that's what I mean.

SOCRATES: Well, what I think, in fact, is that orators have the least "power" of all in the state.

POLOS: So! And yet they can have anyone killed as they wish – like the tyrants. And don't they take away people's wealth and chase them out of the city – when and however they wish?

SOCRATES: They certainly do, yes! But I'm not sure whether you are stating something or asking me a question.

POLOS: As you can hear, I'm asking you a question.

SOCRATES: Fine, my friend, then you are asking me two things at once.

POLOS: Why two?

SOCRATES: You asked: don't the orators do what they want? And you asked: don't they do as they please? To my mind there are two questions here. And I maintain: they have as good as no power in the state –

because, while they do what they please they don't do what they really want.

POLOS: And I'm supposed to be patient!

SOCRATES *insisting*: This is my thesis: they don't do what they really want. Please prove to me the contrary.

POLOS: Haven't you already admitted that they do what they please?

SOCRATES: Yes. And I'm still admitting it.

POLOS: Then they must be doing what they want!

SOCRATES: No, I say!

POLOS: Although they are doing what they please?

SOCRATES: Yes.

POLOS: But Socrates, those are completely nonsensical, absurd notions.

SOCRATES: Spare me your abuse, Polos. If you don't manage to show me by your questions that I am wrong then perhaps try to do it by answering my questions.

POLOS: Good, then I will answer your questions. I must find out what your real meaning is.

SOCRATES: If one does something because of something else, one does not want the thing one is actually doing but the thing which is the reason for doing it. Is that true, in general?

POLOS: Yes.

SOCRATES: So, if we kill someone or banish them and

take away their wealth – don't we do it because we believe it is better for us to do it than not to do it?

POLOS: Certainly.

SOCRATES: Therefore, for the sake of good we do all that when we do it?

POLOS: Yes.

SOCRATES: We don't simply just kill, banish and take away wealth; instead we only want it insofar as it is good for us. If it were not good, then we would not do it. For we want – you said it yourself! – we want the good. Whereas we don't want the bad. True?
Silence.
Polos, am I right or am I wrong?
Silence.
Why are you not answering?

POLOS *pettishly*: You are right.

SOCRATES: And so we are in agreement. Now, when someone, whether a tyrant or a orator kills people or banishes them or robs them of their possessions thinking it is good for him to do so, although it is really the opposite – this person is indeed doing what he pleases – or not?

POLOS: Yes.

SOCRATES: But is he not also doing what he wants? When it is, in fact, bad for him?
Silence.
Why are you saying nothing?

POLOS: All right. So it looks as though he is not doing what he wants to do.

SOCRATES: But now, if – as you yourself maintain – if power is something good: has such a person really great power in the state?

POLOS: No!

SOCRATES: Then I am right: a man who in a state does what he pleases perhaps does not have much power – because he does not do what he really wants!

POLOS *relinquishing the objective tone of discussion*: As if you, Socrates, did not prefer to have freedom to do what you please in the state rather than not to have it. And as if you would not envy one who had power to kill as he wished, to confiscate possessions, to lock up in jail …

SOCRATES: Do you mean, to do these things justly or unjustly?

POLOS: Who cares? Is such a person not to be envied in any case?

SOCRATES *very seriously*: Polos, don't say such wanton things!

POLOS: Why?

SOCRATES: We should not envy those who are unenviable! They are to be pitied; for they are unhappy.

POLOS: The one who is unhappy and to be pitied is surely the one who suffers an unjust death.

SOCRATES: No, Polos, not as much as the one who imposes this death. And less to be pitied than one who is justly put to death.

POLOS: Why is that?

SOCRATES: Because there is nothing worse than doing wrong.

POLOS: But isn't it still worse to suffer injustice?

SOCRATES: No, certainly not!

POLOS: And what about you? Would you really want to suffer injustice than to commit it?

SOCRATES: I wouldn't want either. But if I had to choose, I would rather suffer wrong than do it.

POLOS: Any child could show that you are on the wrong track.

SOCRATES: In that case I would thank the child. And I will thank you, too, if you free me from my folly. So, enjoy helping a friend – by refuting his arguments.

POLOS: Good, Socrates. I don't need to speak about remote things. In recent days there are events which everyone knows about and which are a proof that there are people who commit crimes and yet are happy.

SOCRATES: And what kind of men would they be?

POLOS: You see, for example, how Archélaos rules over Macedonia?

SOCRATES: I don't see it, but I know about it from hearsay.

POLOS: Do you think he is happy or unhappy?

SOCRATES: I don't know, Polos! I have nothing to do with the man.

POLOS: Then you will also say that you don't know whether the Great King is happy or not.

SOCRATES: Of course I will say that. And rightly so. Because I don't know anything about his justice.

POLOS: So that, for you, is the criterion of happiness?

SOCRATES: Yes, dear friend. I say the good man is happy. But the man who does wrong – he is the one I call unhappy.

POLOS: And so Archélaos is also unhappy in your opinion?

SOCRATES: If he commits injustice – yes!

POLOS *attempting superior irony*: Well, that he "commits injustice" – that can be said! He didn't have even the slightest claim to the throne. If justice were done Archélaos would today be the slave of Alcetas – and then, as you maintain, he would be happy. But now, as is well known, he has committed the greatest crimes – without noticing that he has thereby become deeply unhappy. First he had his uncle and then Alcetas killed and then, straightaway, his cousin. And then, a short time afterwards he missed another opportunity of becoming happy: he threw the rightful heir to the throne into a well, his own brother, a seven-year-old boy. So – and now he has become the most unhappy of all Macedonians! I hear that there are even people in Athens who don't want to change places with Archélaos, a certain Socrates, for example!

SOCRATES *after a brief silence*: So that is the proof you have promised? – I don't accept a word of it.
The Young Woman has for a while been attempting to speak.

PROFESSOR *laying the text aside and turning to the Young Woman*: Doctor, you have an objection, I see. You don't agree?

YOUNG WOMAN: No, not an objection! On the contrary! I fully agree. But a "dumb question:" who is Archélaos? What is it with these crimes of his? Is all of that historical? Is he a contemporary of Plato?

PROFESSOR: Not of Plato, but he is a contemporary of Socrates. Both Archélaos and Socrates died in the same year: 399.

Archélaos was the founder of Macedonian military power, which, as we know, would then, two generations later, set up a world empire: Alexander's empire. In Archélaos's court the splendour must have been unbelievable. For example, the greatest painter in Greece was there: Zeuxis; and Euripides, the tragedian – both were summoned and brought there from far away: by none other than Archélaos!

YOUNG WOMAN: But that is all as it should be! It is marvelous!

PROFESSOR: But it is true that this same man is a common criminal. Coming to the throne by committing numerous murders – through treacherous murders of the worst, lowest kind.

WRITER *has meantime gone searching the bookshelves and has taken down a lexicon volume which he holds open in his hand*: Things like this are easily forgotten – in the course of history. Here there is only this *he reads it out*: "Archélaos, Macedonian king" etc, etc., and then: "his achievements were his promotion of Greek culture, building of cities and roads." That's it!

JOURNALIST: Road building. Autobahns. The classical alibi for dictators.

PROFESSOR: This alibi is not acceptable to everyone. Plato, for instance, makes no mention of Archélaos's cultural achievements! *Turning to the Young Woman:* So that was it. Happy?

YOUNG WOMAN: Yes. I'm really sorry.

PROFESSOR: But you are playing your role excellently! *He picks up the text again.* So Socrates says he is amazed that this Archélaos argument should be proof of anything: "I don't accept a word of it!"

SOCRATES: So you think it is possible for someone to commit acts of injustice and at the same time to be happy?

POLOS: Certainly!

SOCRATES: And I say to you: that is impossible! That is the one point on which we disagree. Next: should the criminal still be happy if he receives the appropriate punishment?

POLOS: No, of course not! That, precisely, would make him unhappy.

SOCRATES: But, my dear Polos, I, for my part, say: anyone who commits acts of injustice is unhappy in any case. But he is unhappier if he does not atone for his crimes. And he is less unhappy if he is called to account by gods and men and receives his punishment.

POLOS: Dear Socrates! Are your arguments not already refuted by the fact that the things you are maintaining would not occur to anyone else? Ask anyone else who is present!

SOCRATES: Don't have me hold a vote! I, at least, am firmly convinced that all men, not just myself, but you and everyone else, think that acting unjustly is worse than suffering injustice and that not being punished is worse than being punished.

POLITICIAN *who has been becoming impatient for some time*: Now this has become completely unreal! Excuse me interrupting you. But you seem – sorry, Socrates seems to have lost touch with reality. Doctor, don't you, too, want to protest? That is your role in this. Do you not think that reality has now simply evaporated?

YOUNG WOMAN *hesitating at first but then very firmly*: No, I don't think that at all. Of course, Socrates's last sentence is a provocation. The formulation is extreme. But – unrealistic, fanciful, or just an exaggeration? I don't think we can say that. Socrates is simply right. – But I would still like to ask him: what has happened to oratory? That hasn't been mentioned for a long time. Power – justice – happiness: those are quite new themes!

PROFESSOR: Excellent! This question hits the bullseye! But it is not easy to answer. Not with a few sentences. Strictly speaking, the whole "Gorgias" dialogue is the answer. – You say, "quite new themes." And you are right. But the relationship of the new themes to the old theme "oratory" is very close. On one side of the coin you have happiness, justice, truth – three things which belong together. But the other side of the same coin also has three things which belong together: one of them is … oratory, that is, the use of words in isolation from objective truth; the second is uninhibited exercise of power; the third is despair.

YOUNG WOMAN: Good heavens! That is all very cryptic! The average reader can't possibly decipher that!

PROFESSOR: And yet it is completely plausible! The dialogue process moves from the symptom of the sickness to its centre. After that there is no further talk of the symptom.

JOURNALIST: And what is the symptom?

PROFESSOR: The symptom is oratory!

JOURNALIST: So, journalism! Thanks very much!

PROFESSOR: Sorry! No. The symptom is the oratory of the sophists, degenerate journalism, of course! Irresponsible use of words. Plato's thesis could be formulated as follows: if in the public life of a state the tone is set by an oratory for which the true facts are of no interest then this state is corrupt. How relevant these things are today becomes clear as soon as, instead of "oratory," I speak of a "journalism" that primarily does not say anything but has a particular aim – which is true both of political propaganda and of business advertising. Instead of "oratory" I could also say "entertainment," meaning the attractive, empty offerings which these days are showered on people. And, by the way, the old-fashioned concept of "flattery" is realized here: you tell people what they want to hear so as to make them do something – for example, to buy and to pay.
So that is Plato's meaning: if such things define the foreground and the outer aspect of communal life then the innards of the social body are sick. Behind the scenes there is the naked battle for power.

YOUNG WOMAN: But that is your interpretation, isn't it? Nothing is said directly about that? Oratory is no longer under discussion!

PROFESSOR: But it is. On one occasion Socrates – of course, we can't read all of it – Socrates speaks to Polos again expressly about oratory. It is, admittedly, a very special kind of oratory – silent, internal. What is the point – Socrates more or less says – of this self-justification no matter what; this skill in talking your way out of trouble, this use of words to avoid punishment, the absolute need to be successful – what is the good of all that: if the punishment frees us of our injustice! Perhaps oratory should be used for the opposite – for self-accusation!

POLITICIAN *becoming impatient*: I repeat: now the thing is becoming unreal!

PROFESSOR: Yes, of course it is approaching a border. One can ask, however, the border of what? I would say: the border between the average and the heroic life.
You say: it is becoming unreal. In our dialogue Callicles says something like that; that's where his role begins. *He opens the text at the passage in question.* Well, he doesn't say "unreal;" he says: "a joke."

POLITICIAN: And he is right. Let me see.
The Professor hands him the text and shows him the passage.

POLITICIAN: Yes! That's exactly my opinion!
He reads it to himself for a moment and then he takes on, step by step, the role of Callicles, with whom he increasingly identifies himself.

CALLICLES: Tell me, Socrates, how are we to understand this: do you mean it seriously or are you making a joke? If you mean it seriously and if what you are saying is true – then the whole of human life is being completely turned upside down. For what we in fact do is exactly the opposite of what we should do – if we were to follow you!

SOCRATES: It's not a question of following me, Callicles. It is philosophy that says such surprising things. So you have to refute philosophy! Now you have to prove something. You have to prove that acting unjustly and remaining unpunished are not the worst things that can befall a person. If you cannot prove that, then, dear Callicles, Callicles does not agree with you and he remains in conflict with you for the whole of his life. For my part, my dear man, I would find it easier to bear if the majority of people were in conflict with me than if I myself, within myself, were in conflict with myself; if I were divided within myself.

CALLICLES: You are sounding like a mob orator. Besides, you are playing a cunning trick. You are mixing up two things. One thing is based on nature, and the other is right or wrong as determined by man-made laws. Nature tells us it is far worse to suffer injustice than to commit it; according to our man-made laws – apparently – it is the other way round. But anyone who is really a man will not tolerate being treated unjustly. That is more something for a slave, who, in any case, would be better off dead than alive because he is unable to protect either himself or anyone he loves from insult and maltreatment. And it is precisely the weaklings and the large throngs that think up statutes and laws. And so they say it is "unjust" to do any-thing disadvantageous others. But nature proves the opposite, namely, that justice is when the better person has the advantage over the worse person and the more capable over the less capable. Otherwise, with what right would Xerxes have gone to war with Greece? That corresponds to nature, and, by God, also to the law, namely, the law of nature – of course, not to the law we ourselves have thought out for ourselves. This law we have made brings us to the point that we control and tame, from childhood onwards, the best and the strongest, as we do lions, and we are continually telling them that everything has to be shared "equally:" that this is "good" and "just." But when the right man comes, bursting with natural strength, he shakes all of that off, frees himself, tramples on all our paragraphs, all this trickery, this verbiage and the whole pile of unnatural statutes. From being a slave he climbs up to be the master – of us all! Then it becomes crystal-clear what is meant by: natural law! That's the way it is. You, too, will see that if you could finally decide to give up philosophy and apply yourself to more serious things! I do admit: if one is preoccupied with it in one's early years, and in moderation, philosophy does have its attraction. But if a man is not free of it soon enough it can become a disaster for him, because everything one needs to know if one is to be of consequence in the community is naturally foreign to him and unfamiliar. When I see a man in his mature years still preoccupied with philosophy – well, dear Socrates, such a man deserves to be beaten: that's my opinion. – Can you call it "wisdom" when a person is not able to fend for himself?

In plain language: you can punch such a man in the face with impunity!

SOCRATES *smiling, beginning calmly after a short pause*: You are quite right. There is no more important question than what makes one to be a real man, and what he must do, and how long, in his later years as well as in his early years. And believe me: if I am not on the right track with my life as I now lead it, it is not intentional but due to ignorance. So, please continue to warn me and to put me right! But first, what was your opinion regarding what is right "on the basis of nature"? Didn't you say that it is right for the stronger man to take the possessions of the weaker and that the better man should rule over the worse man and the capable should have the advantage over the less capable?

CALLICLES: Yes, that's what I said, and I still say it.

SOCRATES: But you don't consider that two are "better" than one? Or that your slaves are "better" than you because they are stronger than you? When you say "better" and "stronger" perhaps you mean more intelligent.

CALLICLES: Yes! That's what I mean. And that is the law of nature: the better and more intelligent man has to rule the incapable.

SOCRATES: But tell me now: in what must a man be stronger and know more if he is justified in getting more than the rest?

CALLICLES: I mean those who understand something about politics and are good at it. They rightly have the advantage over the others; they, the rulers, over those who are ruled.

SOCRATES: And ... must they be in command of themselves – or only of others?

CALLICLES: In command of themselves? What do you mean by that?

SOCRATES: Oh, nothing particularly unusual – just what is normally meant: that one exercises self-discipline, and has one's moods and desires under control.

CALLICLES: You really are quite simple! Do you mean these imbeciles who "exercise moderation"?

SOCRATES: Of course I mean them! There can be no mis-understanding about that.

CALLICLES: Anyone who is ruled, no matter by whom, cannot be happy. Now I will tell you plainly what is naturally beautiful and right: a person who really wants to live must make his wishes and desires grow as big and strong as possible. And then he has to be in a position to satisfy them with all the strength and in-telligence at his command. But most people don't manage that! Socrates, you are always saying you seek the truth. But this is what truth looks like: to be able to enjoy without hindrance and in so doing to have all the means and aids at one's disposal – that is what is meant by "good" and being happy! All your lovely words and the unnatural human norms and rules – all of that is only wind and idle chatter.

SOCRATES: Well, Callicles, you are not exactly shy – the way you let rip without any inhibition! What others only think but don't have the confidence to say you have no problem in saying. – So, it is not at all true that a happy person is one who has absolutely no needs?

CALLICLES: In that case, stones and the dead would be the happiest! No, you only have a pleasant life if you grab for yourself as much as possible.

SOCRATES: That sounds more like the life of a duck!

CALLICLES *not listening at all, continues unflustered*: Yes, that's what I mean: to have all the desires and to satisfy them! That is the only way to enjoy life.

SOCRATES: Does "pleasant" therefore also mean "good"? Are these one and the same? Or are there things which are pleasant but not good?

CALLICLES: No, they are one and the same.

SOCRATES: Have you never seen an idiot who feels contented with life?

CALLICLES: What's the point of this?

SOCRATES: Never mind. Just answer.

CALLICLES: Yes, I have.

SOCRATES: Next: you would also have seen a clever man who is contented with life – and one who is discontented?

CALLICLES: Yes.

SOCRATES: Then which of them had more contentment or also more displeasure – the clever man or the idiot?

CALLICLES: There will hardly have been much difference.

SOCRATES: Good. That's all I need. Next: in battle, when the enemy retreats, who is happier about it – the cowardly or the brave?

CALLICLES: Both, equally – or almost equally.

SOCRATES: So, you are saying it yourself: people feel contentment and displeasure more or less equally – whether they are clever or stupid, brave or cowardly?

CALLICLES: Yes.

SOCRATES: The clever and the brave – those are surely the good! And the cowards and the ignorant – those are the bad?

CALLICLES: Yes.

SOCRATES: It follows that the good and the bad, both, are almost equally good and almost equally bad?

CALLICLES: For heaven's sake – what are you driving at now?

SOCRATES: That, my dear Callicles, is nothing but the inescapable conclusion one arrives at when one starts by saying that the pleasant and the good are one and the same thing.

CALLICLES: I've been listening to you a long time like this and I am saying "yes" – because I notice that you enjoy it as soon as someone concedes something if only in fun. You don't really think I wanted to deny that pleasure is sometimes good but also sometimes bad!?

SOCRATES: All right! A thing is good, then, when it does one good? And it is bad when it does harm?

CALLICLES: Yes.

SOCRATES: But when it does one good one has to make sure to have it?

CALLICLES: Naturally.

SOCRATES: But if it is harmful one must fend it off?

CALLICLES: Of course! That's obvious!

SOCRATES: Then one must, as with everything else, choose the pleasant for the sake of the good – not the good for the sake of pleasure?

CALLICLES: Of course.

SOCRATES: But is everyone in a position to distinguish which of the pleasant things are good and which are bad? Or can only an expert do that?

CALLICLES: Naturally!

SOCRATES *with a concluding gesture*: So then we are agreed on the following: there is the good and there is the pleasant; and one is not the same as the other. The pleasant, when we have it, gives us a feeling of well-being and makes us joyful; the good, when we have it, makes us good. Agreed?

CALLICLES: Yes.

SOCRATES: Excellent! But now, what about the art of speaking – as practiced in front of the people, in Athens and elsewhere? Do you think the practitioners of the word always have the good of their citizens in mind – or do they want to say only pleasant things to them, whether the outcome is good or bad?

CALLICLES: That can't be answered in a single sentence.

SOCRATES: Then tell me what I should do. Please, be very precise. Should I, like a doctor, aim to make Athenians healthier, and therefore better – or should I, like a slave, tell them what they want to hear?
Callicles is silent.
Tell me the truth.
Silence.
The honest truth!

CALLICLES *after some hesitation*: All right: tell them what they want to hear!

SOCRATES: Oh, you noble man! You want me to be a flatterer?

CALLICLES *with a threatening overtone in his voice*: You seem to feel very sure of yourself, Socrates! As if nothing could happen to you. As if you lived out of harm's way.

SOCRATES: Then I would really be a fool – if I didn't see that in our city anything can happen to anybody. – And it would not be a surprise if in such a case I should have to die. Should I tell you why I am prepared for that?

CALLICLES: Well?

SOCRATES: Imagine a doctor, taken to court by a cook – you know, a confectioner of sweets, and defending himself in a courtroom of children. This is the way I will be condemned. Imagine what this defendant could say in his defense in such a courtroom. The prosecutor would say, for example: This man, my dear children has done a lot of bad things to you with cutting and burning and bitter-tasting medicine; he makes you go hungry and thirsty! But I, I have done good things to you with delicacies and sweets. – Now, what is the doctor to say in such a situation? And if he were to speak the truth: "All of that, dear children, I have done only for the good of your health" – what an uproar do you think would come from these judges?

CALLICLES: One can easily imagine.

SOCRATES: Well, that's exactly what would happen to me if I had to appear before the court. I will not be able to boast that I have brought them advantages – which is all that they value as good. On the contrary – as regards the advantages, I neither applaud those who create them nor those who enjoy them. And so I will have to accept whatever is decided about me.

CALLICLES: And you consider that is all in order – that in such a situation there is nothing one can do?

SOCRATES: Yes, I consider that is all in order – on the supposition that one has already done what can be done, namely, by not having done wrong either to man or to the gods, either in word or in deed. That is the best way there is to help oneself. If it should turn out that I was not in a position to help myself or another in this way then I would be ashamed. And if I had to go to my death for that reason because I am not capable of that flattering way with words – then, believe me, I would find it easy to die.

Nobody fears actual dying – unless he has lost all understanding and courage. What one fears is wrongdoing. The worst thing that can happen to us is this: for the soul to come into Hades laden with guilt. If you like, I'll tell you an old story about this.

CALLICLES *not very enthusiastic*: All right – if you absolutely must!

SOCRATES: Then listen. You will think the story is a fairy tale; I think it is the truth! And the reason for telling it is that it is true.
He reflects for a brief moment and then begins.
From time immemorial man was subject to the divine law: one who has led his life in justice and piety will, after his death, be brought to the Isles of the Blessed. There he will live, far from all suffering and in perfect bliss. But one who has led an unjust and impious life will come to the place of atonement and punishment, called Tartarus. It follows from this, it seems to me, that after death, after the separation of body and soul, both body and soul will remain the same as they were before death – almost unchanged. Regarding the soul, when it has left the body, everything will be revealed: not only what it is by nature but also what has later been inscribed in it by the person's own doing. And when it now comes before the judge it could be that nothing healthy is found but that, instead, everywhere scars as from the lash – the results of perjury and injustice; everything about the soul is misshapen as a result of lies and boasting; nothing is straight because it has lived without truth. Then the judge sends it straight into shameful imprisonment; and there it suffers what it has deserved. The persons whose wrongdoing can be cured will be brought on the road of recovery through punishment. But in Hades, no less than on earth, this benefit will accrue to him only

through suffering and pain: there is no other way of becoming quit of injustice. – But those who through their irredeemable crimes have become irredeemable themselves must suffer the most fearsome tortures, being held up eternally in the underworld as a specter and as a frightening example to all evildoers who arrive there.

If Polos's report is true then Archélaos and all those who, like him, rule by violence will be amongst them. *After a slight pause, beginning again:* Now and then the judge will meet a soul of another kind, which, honoring the gods, has lived for the truth – the soul of a man, for example, my dear Callicles, of a philosophical man, who all his life, away from the empty hurly burly of the world, has followed his own lights. The judge will be pleased with this soul and send him to the Isles of the Blessed.

As for myself, Callicles, I believe in the truth of this story, and I intend to bring my soul before the judge in the best possible state. I am not concerned with honor and applause from the many. Instead, I will strive for truth, and try, as far as possible, to live a good life – and when the time comes – to die a good death. But I will call on all other men, wherever I can, and now on you, to take on this life and this struggle which I consider greater than all battles for power in the world.

In the following Socrates no longer addresses Callicles but the spectators.

But I suspect you think all that is nothing but old wives' tales, not worth worrying about. That would be even quite understandable – except that, with all our research, we are in no position to discover anything that is better and more true! Of all the statements we have made there is only one that has remained intact: to do wrong is far more to be feared than to suffer wrong; and we have, above all, to try not to seem good, but to be good.

For a time silence reigns. – It is clear that the Young Woman is deeply impressed, even affected. – The Politician goes on smoking his cigar, somewhat nervously; from time to time he moves his head from one side to the other; he shows both scepticism and respect. The Writer leans back in his chair, seeming to enjoy the situation, and remains in this posture without moving. He is clearly avoiding commitment to any particular view. – The Journalist, who seems to be the least affected, ignores the painful silence that is developing. He crosses the room, takes a cigarette, which he – plainly without ceremony – lights and immediately energetically stubs out in the ashtray. He looks at the Professor and shakes his head aggressively. – The Professor looks with interest from one to the other. He is slightly amused, but serious. Then he turns to the Journalist:

PROFESSOR: May one ask what you are not satisfied with? What objections do you have?

JOURNALIST: Oh, very many! – Above all: this story at the end … I am also amazed that something like that is to be found word for word in Plato; it all seems so familiar …

PROFESSOR: Is that an objection? After all …

JOURNALIST: Of course not. I have objections of a quite different kind.
First: what is the point of this story? Does it have anything to do with what we were discussing previously?

PROFESSOR: I think there is an answer to this question. – And "secondly"?

JOURNALIST: Don't you find that this pious story about heaven and earth is in no way binding? At least, it is anything but an argument!

PROFESSOR *smiles as he goes back a few pages in the text and reads aloud*: "You, Callicles, consider that a fairy tale; I take it to be the truth." – Plato was obviously aware of the objection.

JOURNALIST: That's as it may be. But he doesn't answer it. For a moment he simply stops arguing philosophically. Suddenly something quite different is said.

YOUNG WOMAN: But who says it always has to be "philosophical"? Are there not other arguments as well?

PROFESSOR *surprised*: Very good! That is excellent. That is one of my pet theories: Plato is not at all interested in "philosophy." And probably that is exactly what is philosophical about him.

WRITER *casually throwing in*: Aha. Pascal: "the true philosopher makes fun of philosophy." Is that what you mean?

PROFESSOR *hesitantly*: Perhaps! Something like that. But no. For Plato it's a different thing.

JOURNALIST: Lovely! Plato is not interested in philosophy. Then what is he interested in?

PROFESSOR: He's interested in the answer. He is interested in the most accurate and the most comprehensive answer possible: to one question.

JOURNALIST: To what kind of question?

PROFESSOR: In this case, to the question: why must a person unconditionally be just even when in being so he is risking his life? Every possible answer to this is examined – until the last, the most extreme one is produced: the argument based on judgment after death.

JOURNALIST: But "judgment after death" – You must admit: that is not a philosophical argument – *to the Young Woman with slightly ironical accentuation* – provided one means by philosophy "thinking for yourself."

PROFESSOR: But philosophy does also mean not excluding any available information!

JOURNALIST: But are we really dealing with information? Above all, is it attainable, that is, is it verifiable? Besides, who takes responsibility for it?

PROFESSOR: Of course, you are right. Strictly speaking, this is where Plato's authorship ends. The author of this story – again I would say, this myth, about the judgment of the dead – is neither Socrates nor Plato.

JOURNALIST *with slight annoyance and astonishment*: Then who is it? Who else?

PROFESSOR: Plato doesn't give any name. He says: wisdom of the ancients. But the "ancients" remain anonymous. In tradition handed down to us there is a lot of anonymity. Tradition – yes, that is probably the right word; basically we are dealing with "sacred tradition." But that is a new topic …
The Politician looks demonstratively at his watch.

PROFESSOR *to the Politician*: Yes, yes, you are right. We are getting into grey areas. But don't worry. *Turning to the Journalist again*: At this point we don't have to involve ourselves with "tradition" – fortunately. The main point is that Plato accepts it, tradition, sacred tradition – and not just as "information," but as truth, inviolable truth.

JOURNALIST: All right. But "sacred tradition"? I have no idea what you mean by that in the concrete. One thing is clear to me [and, I presume, to you too]: that it has nothing to do with thought, knowledge, science, rational illumination of facts; and, likewise, it has nothing to do with philosophy!

PROFESSOR: Careful, careful! It has nothing to do with philosophy ...? Well, certainly it is something different. If we try to place it in the categories we are familiar with – yes, I would say: sacred tradition has to do with theology; we are in fact dealing with something like theology – even here in the Gorgias dialogue!

JOURNALIST *thinking he has at last found the telling argument*: Voilà: theology! That's exactly where my argument was heading! Theology appears as the answer to everything!
The Professor nods in agreement, obviously enjoying the debate.

JOURNALIST *in an aggressive tone*: Apparently that is of no significance to you? But didn't you assure us right at the beginning that this Gorgias of Plato is full of modernity?

PROFESSOR *very quickly and energetically, but without sharpness in his tone*: Yes, I did say that, and I still say it now! – But, of course, you find that absurd...

The Writer raises his hands imploringly; he wants to mediate but also change the subject.

WRITER: Could we not agree on the following? *Complex gesturing to introduce his idea:* This "story" – whatever way it is to be interpreted and no matter who the author is [I would say: of course it is Plato! Who else could it be? Plato is the maker of myths, the writer!].

PROFESSOR *more to himself*: Myths are not made! A real myth …

YOUNG WOMAN: … is like a revelation, like "the word of God:" that is your meaning! I sense it.

PROFESSOR: But do you also "sense" how unbelievably difficult it is, in this context, to say anything with some sort of precision?

WRITER *persisting*: Whatever about all of that – Sorry! But this story is absolutely vital! It comes at the end, doesn't it? Naturally, Plato considers that Socrates is right and we are left in no doubt about it. But he could be a thousand times right, yet he remains isolated. He does not enjoy the slightest success. But then, then comes the mythical story. In his isolation he suddenly encounters this new metaphysical horizon which has been hidden until now! And behold! The world has been put back on its hinges! Form takes on its perfect, seamless shape. The dialogue becomes a work of art!

PROFESSOR *who has been accompanying the last sentences with a good-natured, ironic nodding of the head*: Poésie pure!

WRITER *not wanting to be put off his stride*: This is precisely what I think is marvelous about the myth of the final judgment: that he is successful with it! It is simply the finale, without which the symphony would have remained a fragment. – Is there anyone who disagrees? *The Journalist energetically shoots up his hand, and then with an air of authority:*

JOURNALIST: Yes, there is.

PROFESSOR: I don't dispute it! – However, I don't agree with you – and you wouldn't expect me to. I am not happy … with this demand for a, what shall I say, false unanimity, or, let's say, a unanimity about something that is not the essential point.

WRITER *resignedly*: And what is the essential point?

PROFESSOR: Certainly not "formal excellence!"

WRITER: But?

PROFESSOR: The essential point is whether it applies; the essential point is truth. But the only question that a person versed in history is sure not to ask is the question about truth. That is, of course, a slight exaggeration – but to the extent that it is true we would, to the same extent, be incapable of reading Plato in the way he wants to be read. He, namely, is concerned with only one thing: the uncovering and opening up of reality, especially as regards human beings; that is, he is concerned with the truth. His friends should be concerned about this and not about him. In his farewell speech in the death cell this is what Socrates implores of his companions – who, by the way, do not show much understanding. Only one of his pupils and disciples understood anything: Plato! And as a heading to his own work there is a kind of Socratic challenge:

don't be fascinated by form in language and in writing, by the colorful interplay of influences, challenges and dependencies. What is decisive is something quite different .... And this different thing – *he makes a gesture of resignation* – oh, you just have to quote that one sentence from the "Phaedo." It can't be said any clearer: 'Don't worry about Socrates, worry about the truth!'

THE SYMPOSIUM

Characters

SOCRATES

AGATHON

ARISTOPHANES

ERYXIMACHUS

PAUSANIAS

PHAEDRUS

ALCIBIADES

ARISTODEMUS

SPEAKER

The action is not restricted to any particular place or time. It does not have to be in Athens of the 5th century B.C. It could be in one of today's major cities.

The Scene

The living room of a modern lavishly built house. The modernity should not be so exactly defined as to prevent the suggestion of a certain timelessness. The numerous pieces of furniture are loosely arranged: small tables, arm-chairs, padded benches, stools – all lightly built so that without much fuss a conversation group can easily be formed and changed. Several standard lamps; books and pictures on the walls; a couple of sculptures. On the left the room opens onto an atrium through which the newly arriving guests enter. Towards the back there is an additional spacious room the full width of the area, separated by a curtain stretching from the ceiling to the floor. The curtain is not so tightly woven as to obscure the spectator's view. It is only half closed. In front of it is a buffet table on which are numerous dishes. In the glass wall on the right there is a wide door which leads to a garden terrace. The door is open.

The characters

A circle of intellectuals who know one another or are friends is gathering: a doctor, a writer, people interested in literature. The attire of the circle should be fairly varied – quite modern and perhaps in some cases fashionable – but not, in its detail, identifiable with any particular decade. There are also two or three staff in white formal uniform which does not, however, have military overtones. It could belong in the present or in the past two hundred years; in Europe or in India. Along with the characters appearing on the screen there is a speaker who remains invisible.

SOCRATES, *a little more than fifty years old. Dressed rather ineptly for a day of celebration [for example, a somewhat oversized old-fashioned cravat]. His manner and demeanour explain why he can be both misunderstood by the others as, shall we say, an odd character, and also, because of his existential seriousness, admired and enthusiastically honored as a brilliant teacher of philosophy.*

AGATHON, *a famous writer who is hosting the evening in his house. About thirty-five years old. Dressed with great care, very fashionable, but deliberately informal; he could be given a slight hint of foppishness. With social graces and in command of the situation. In every respect not only literary but representing the most up-to-date avant-garde.*

ARISTOPHANES, *the writer of comedies, is a specially honored guest. Full of breadth and sonorous vitality. For the most part quiet; only occasionally booming laughter and sharp comments. There is a tragic seriousness hidden behind his speech which is characterized by the grotesque. He is dressed in a somewhat old-fashioned way and untidily; the carelessness of a man who is sure of himself; he is not concerned with current fashion. Somewhat older than Socrates.*

ERYXIMACHUS, *a doctor with something of the health-apostle about him. He gives genteel society recipes for living in accordance with "nature." Pedantically dressed. A suggestion of choosing to dress in his own way; perhaps sandals, or a Schiller collar, or breeches. But the loner aspect should not be exaggerated. Around forty-five years old. Glasses. Strongly didactic tone.*

PAUSANIAS, a *well-to-do man of about fifty. Educated in literature. Many-sided interests. Elegantly dressed. He likes* to speak about ideals but knows that, in reality, when he does so no one takes him seriously. Ironic relativism.

PHAEDRUS, *a young artist and literary type, in a roll-neck pullover. His passionate side can be seen even in the way he wears his hair. Romantic but not in the sense that he entertains vague feelings of bliss. More drawn to the heroic. He searches for words, then expresses himself with absoluteness and explosive vigor.*

ALCIBIADES, *the same age as Agathon. Loud, spoilt, used to success. No shame and "capable of anything." Fashionably dressed but in a certain disarray. A political demagogue whose future destructive behavior can already be anticipated.*

ARISTODEMUS, *a very young student unreservedly devoted to Socrates. Dress: outdoor shirt, blue jeans, sandals. He could seem out of place here, but it must remain plausible that, in Plato's opinion, he has good prospects. During the whole evening he has to be seen as a passionately attentive listener.*

As soon as the title appears on the screen, music is heard. It has the function, above all, of creating an atmosphere of indefinable timelessness with a sort of surrealistic sense of time and place. I am thinking of cheerful melodic sound structures, but, of course, ones which do not evoke associations with Classical or other familiar themes. No piano or violin amongst the instruments, but rather cembalo, lyre, flute, percussion. From time to time the music becomes louder and the characters interrupt their conversation to listen. It remains open whether in the atrium, for instance, the music is made by invisible musicians or whether it comes over the loudspeaker.

At lights-up the whole space is lit. Agathon gives a discreet signal to one of the staff, who then goes into the room at the back. Eryximachus, a trifle too ceremoniously, carries a large bunch of grapes held out in front of him, and Phaedrus, visibly somewhat bored, from time to time puts in his mouth one of the nuts he is holding in his hand. They approach the open terrace door and remain standing in faltering conversation.

[Inaudible dialogue; drowned out by the music and the speaker's commentary:

ERYXIMACHUS: From where a doctor stands the world looks very different. Very different. Can you imagine that?

PHAEDRUS *friendly, distracted*: Sure, yes, I understand.

ERYXIMACHUS: The world looks very different, but above all man does. Very different!

Pausanias and Aristophanes have remained seated in the corner of the room down stage. Pausanias carefully chooses a cigar from the various kinds offered by one of the staff and lights it with elaborate ceremony, while Aristophanes is clinically dissecting an apple.
One of the servants quickly and quietly cleans the tables; crockery, cutlery and serviettes are taken out on an elegantly shaped table trolley.
The servant sent by Agathon into the back room returns and goes around, consciously avoiding all noise, and lights the lamps.

SPEAKER: Plato's "Symposium!" The title is, of course, very old, but it is not quite accurate. The feasting is already over. Also, the Greek name "symposion" –

"drinking session," is, as will become clear, not really apt. What we have here is more like a debate, an evening of discussion.

But at the moment it does not yet look as though a discussion will come about. It has not yet even been arranged. Strangely, the main person is missing...

The camera focuses on Agathon, who seems to be straining to listen to the music while at the same time he is thinking of something else entirely. He looks several times at his watch.

... which is why the host is understandably becoming a little nervous. After all, he has put a lot of thought into the invitations for this very special occasion. His latest tragedy – the premiere was the day before yesterday – was not only an outstanding success with the audience; it has, above all, earned him the long-awaited, important literature prize, an event which he wants to celebrate this evening.

The acclaim is already threatening to go slightly to his head; Agathon the person does not seem to be handling it too well; he needs it too much, the acclaim. The camera focuses on Aristophanes. Amazing that Agathon has invited a man like Aristophanes. But it is possibly a question of tactics.

It is not a good idea to get on the wrong side of Aristophanes. But there is no certain recipe for avoiding it; the independence of this man is absolute. Not long ago the Athenians shed tears of laughter about a rather precious Agathon dressed in women's clothing – in a production staged by Aristophanes. It is also well known that Socrates was not spared either. For him it was no better. Worse, if anything.

The camera now shows the whole space again as at the beginning; the clearing up, the pause, the stagnation of the

*situation becomes especially apparent. The music, which re-
turns to the beginning, reinforces this impression.*

As I have indicated, the whole scene has begun to
stagnate; and the waiting has a laming effect. Aristophanes is bored in the company of Pausanias, a cul-
tured pleasure-seeking man about whom not much
more is to be said than that he is rich, "interested," and
turns up everywhere. And what Eryximachus, an odd,
fashionable doctor for rich Athenians is saying to
Phaedrus is something this young man, whose impatience is showing, has already heard a hundred times.

*Eryximachus has signaled to a servant, who brings him a
bowl of water. At first he does not know where to put it, then
places it on a sideboard, dips the bunch of grapes several
times, lets the water drip off and tortuously puts the grapes
one by one into his mouth, after examining each one criti-
cally. Again and again distracted and interrupted by this
process he goes on teaching, though without much vigor.*

ERYXIMACHUS: To take exercise is much more important. Outside in the fresh air, of course.[1] This cannot
be stressed too much. As I always say, medicine and
exercise have to go hand in hand …

*He stops, and with energetic gestures signals to a servant
who is closing the terrace door that he wants it to remain
open. When the servant does not understand him he opens
the door again himself, with a show of stern indulgence.*

*In the meantime, the camera pans slowly over to Pau-
sanias and Aristophanes. Aristophanes is in the middle of
describing a scene from a new comedy he is working on,
moving around the table the pieces of the apple he has cut
up and using them to represent the performing characters.
Pausanias, preoccupied with his cigar, is listening*

distractedly but politely. He only comes to life when he notices a hint of mischief directed against the host.

ARISTOPHANES: So, the messenger says: We need poets in Athens. The good ones are dead, and the living ones are bad. To this, this demon of the underworld replies: First, you realize that no one gets out of here. And second: You have no poets? How come? Don't you have ... *Here he pauses, since he sees Agathon approaching; then he repeats softly and with a suggestive gesture in the direction of Agathon:* No poets? I think you have the very gifted...[2]

PAUSANIAS *interrupting him:* So, your usual witty shot below the belt. *Both laugh. Agathon has meanwhile joined them; he absentmindedly takes a piece of fruit and sits down with them. He looks from time to time at his wristwatch. Aristophanes pushes the pieces of apple to one side and pulls out a short pipe and a somewhat old-fashioned tobacco pouch. Suddenly the servant, who has taken back the fruit dish from Agathon, indicates with a gesture that a new guest seems to have arrived. They all look towards the atrium, from which Aristodemus is ushered into the room by a servant. Aristodemus has resisted with startled gestures and tried to clear up a misunderstanding. He is now standing full of embarrassment at the entrance and looking around helplessly. Agathon has turned to him in some bewilderment. With a quick glance he takes in the strange rigout and mutters, more to himself than anyone, in amazement and slight annoyance:*

AGATHON: Good heavens, who is this? What is it? *Then he suddenly remembers, and with a loud voice pretends to be overjoyed as he approaches Aristodemus.* Yes, of course! Look at you! Naturally! Aristodemus! Excellent! I was looking for you yesterday but you were simply invisible. Yes, yes! No, I know, or I can imagine: you want to discuss something with me. But let us leave that for now; tomorrow will be time enough. This evening you are my guest; you will celebrate with us! No, this has worked out fine! But – tell me, where is your revered lord and master? He can't be far away.

Aristodemus has again and again, in complete embarrassment, tried to explain something and to excuse himself; now he answers, beaming, and then he looks helplessly behind him, pointing to the door:

ARISTODEMUS: I'm wondering myself. Really. I came with him. It was he who invited me. Otherwise I would never have … But suddenly he … yes, he must still be outside …

AGATHON *visibly relieved, to the door-keeper, who has remained standing at the entrance*: Quickly, quickly! Go and look. Welcome him and bring him in immediately. But move!

Aristodemus has again tried to object and to explain. But Agathon takes him by the arm in an energetic and friendly way and leads him into the middle of the room. Agathon gives a signal to a servant, who brings the table trolley with hors d'oeuvres. Aristodemus is given a plate; the servant, spoon and fork in hand, looks at him questioningly. Aristodemus painfully begins to make his choice and keeps on changing his mind at the last moment. Agathon looks at him in amusement.

AGATHON: And now you will take something to eat! [*Inaudible dialogue:*

AGATHON: I imagine you are hungry. As usual, eh?

ARISTODEMUS *laughing unselfconsciously*: Yes! Most of the time I am hungry.

AGATHON: That's more or less what I thought. So, help yourself. This is the specialty of the house. What, you don't want it? All right, then try this?]

SPEAKER: Yes, this boy is a bit strange. But we should not think little of him. For example, in this circle of intelligent men he is the only one who, if he does not altogether understand the greatness of Socrates, at least senses it. What is above all unusual about him is his ability to listen. If, today, we know anything about the conversations held then, we owe this exclusively to him, Aristodemus – as can be seen from reading Plato. *Pausanias and Aristophanes have stood up and are also now slowly approaching. While Pausanias, speaking with almost imperceptible irony, gives Aristodemus some advice:* The olives, superb; no, not the green ones, the black ones, *the door-keeper comes quickly from the atrium to Agathon. It can be seen that, however respectfully, he has already formed his opinion about this and he clearly sees no point in keeping it to himself with exaggerated discretion. Aristophanes puts his hand on Pausanias's arm to silence him and looks over to the door-keeper with an expectant smile which seems to say that he thinks anything is possible but that obviously there are always new surprises. The music has become somewhat louder. The door-keeper is attempting to speak above it. There is a scarcely concealed mocking tone in his voice.*

DOOR-KEEPER: The gentleman is outside. But he won't come in.

AGATHON: Did you ever hear such nonsense!

DOOR-KEEPER *insistently*: The gentleman is standing outside writing something in his notebook. I spoke to him, but he hears and sees nothing.
Aristophanes, in peals of laughter, as much as to say: There you have it! – Agathon, who has become even more annoyed by the tone of the door-keeper which he considers inappropriate, repeats his order with emphasis.

AGATHON: Go on. This is completely absurd. Surely you will find a way to invite a guest into the house.
While the door-keeper, a little too hastily, goes back to the entrance, Socrates enters. It can be seen immediately from his good mood that he has no intention of excusing himself. Everyone looks at him. Aristodemus, in his haste and excitement, gives back to the servant the plate which in the meantime has been filled but untouched, and, beaming, takes some steps towards Socrates. Agathon goes to him quickly and extends his hand.

AGATHON: Socrates! At last! Marvelous!

SOCRATES: Naturally! But yesterday, for the celebration afterwards – well, how many people came: the actors, the stage hands, the chorus? Such occasions don't suit me. But today? I had promised. That was clear, wasn't it? I have even dressed up for it!
The greetings that follow take place with handshakes or just nods. Eryximachus is still busy with his meal of grapes. Socrates puts a friendly arm around the shoulder of Phaedrus, while, accompanied by Agathon, he walks by the trolley with the hors d'oeuvres and by the buffet, his gestures showing admiration but friendly refusal.

[*Inaudible dialogue:*

PAUSANIAS: *pointing to the food*: You've missed a lot,

Socrates. Agathon's cook has excelled himself. It was excellent.

AGATHON: Nothing has been missed. We'll catch up.

SOCRATES: Now, Phaedrus, what have you been doing recently? What new literature is there?

PHAEDRUS: Where should I begin?

SOCRATES *stopping in feigned helplessness in front of the buffet*: What munificence! But it is wasted on me, unfortunately. I know I don't look like an ascetic, but ... *He looks at the bowls with nuts and fruit.* There, the very thing!
With an expansive gesture Agathon invites his guests to take a seat in a circle, leads Socrates to a spacious padded bench and allots him a place to his right. Stools and armchairs are loosely arranged in a circle; between them the servants place small tables. The seating arrangement is such that Phaedrus sits to the right of Socrates and next to him, separated by a larger gap, Pausanias. Then Aristophanes and Eryximachus. Aristodemus has got his plate back and sits down to one side behind Eryximachus so that he can look straight into Socrates's face; at first he devotes himself with fervor to eating.

AGATHON: I think we'll sit down. Well, anywhere you like.]

To Socrates: But you, Socrates, come here and sit beside me – so that I can profit a little from the wise idea that obviously came to you while you were outside there. Otherwise you would not have come in? Am I right?

SOCRATES: It would be nice if wisdom was like that! One would only need to touch another person and it

would flow from the one who is full of wisdom across to the one who is empty. That would be marvelous! For then – yes, then I'd be the lucky one.
Agathon rejects this energetically, threatening in jest.

SOCRATES *not put off*: No, no! My wisdom – a very questionable thing, not much more than a shadow, a dream. But yours! Yours has triumphantly been revealed to more than 30,000 spectators. And you are still so young!

AGATHON *feeling somewhat unsure of himself and slightly irritated*: You are laughing at me; I don't like that. But this thing about wisdom – how to achieve it, if one can achieve it at all, that's something we need to talk about, now, over a glass of wine.
The servants have brought a whole array of glasses of three different kinds, along with several carafes of red and white wine; also dishes with cakes, nuts, and almonds which are served, as required, on small plates.

PAUSANIAS *concerned as he looks at these preparations*: Good heavens! Is this necessary? I must say I don't feel at all inclined to be drinking again. And with this formality – in a circle from left to right? *He makes a counting gesture, referring ironically to the pressure to drink.* What do you all think? We were all there last evening – nearly all.

ARISTOPHANES: Very good! I think that today no one should have to drink. I, too, was out for the count yesterday, completely full. But what does our host say?

AGATHON: I agree entirely. I'm not feeling the best myself.

ERYXIMACHUS *starting into one of his feared lectures*: Yes, this drinking, this intoxication – I mean, from the medical point of view.

All except Socrates and Agathon interrupt him and cut him off with their laughter: Good, fine, stop! We believe you! *Eryximachus is at first slightly affronted, then joins in the laughter and falls silent.*

AGATHON: Good – each according to his taste.

The servants pour the wine for any who want it; the carafes are refilled and placed on side tables. Eryximachus, with some ceremony, refuses the wine; he is served a fruit juice.

ERYXIMACHUS *after several attempts to be heard*: I'd like to make a suggestion. Could we not decide ... to ... I mean ... instead of ...

ARISTOPHANES: Instead of drinking?

ERYXIMACHUS: Yes, instead of that ... do something else? We could surely ... have a discussion. On a particular theme, of course, on which we would have to agree. But not just talk away. Instead, as Pausanias has expressed it: "with formality." Everyone takes his turn; if you like "from left to right."

AGATHON: Not bad. But the theme!

ERYXIMACHUS: Oh, there are plenty of themes. Phaedrus, for example ...

Phaedrus sits bolt upright at the mention of his name; fearing something unpleasant, he looks apprehensively at Eryximachus.

ERYXIMACHUS: I'm not betraying any secrets. Phaedrus is dying to speak about a particular topic. And to hear it discussed. The theme is love – Eros! And knowing him as I do, he will be glad to begin the discussion and be the first to speak.

Phaedrus objects vigorously.

SOCRATES *looking reassuringly across to Phaedrus*: Phaedrus, I think it is a good suggestion. I think we should agree to it. Also to the theme. *Pensively, with ambiguous self-irony:* For myself … I must say that I have no understanding of anything else – except for what concerns love.

Aristophanes bursts out laughing. Socrates does not turn his head but addresses the following to Aristophanes.

And Aristophanes? What does he talk about? Aphrodite! Yes, and Dionysus. – And Phaedrus will chair the discussion. *Phaedrus wants to decline.* No, that's an excellent idea. And of course he has to start – although *turning to Agathon* we are then at a disadvantage; both of us will then be the last ones to speak. But if that is the case we can put up with it.

During the last few minutes the music has become fairly loud.

ERYXIMACHUS *who has already several times looked across with annoyance at the suspected source of the music*: Should we not leave out the music? It's a distraction. *To Agathon:* Of course, it's not for me to say.

AGATHON: You are right.

He makes a sign to a servant, who then goes quickly into the atrium. The music immediately becomes softer and then stops altogether.

ERYXIMACHUS: Thank you. It is easier to understand one another.

Agathon has stood up and gone to the sideboard. After some hesitation he picks up a small bronze figure; with a smile he walks over to Phaedrus and with an encouraging, emphatic gesture puts the figure, which is to indicate whose turn it is to speak, on the table in front of him.

AGATHON: So, Phaedrus, are you ready?
Phaedrus has given up resisting. He tries to concentrate. Then he begins, with a series of vigorous gestures which belie an aggressive attitude controlled only with difficulty, and from which formulated speech does not immediately follow.

PHAEDRUS: Yes, I mean it hasn't been considered properly, not even down to our own day. By anybody!
Pausanias puts on an ironical show of profound respect. Aristophanes ostentatiously interrupts the filling of his pipe and pays serious attention. Socrates turns, with friendly interest, to try and look directly at his neighbor Phaedrus. Eryximachus looks over to his protégé with concern.

PHAEDRUS *who has not yet managed to make a start*: No, never! Not by anyone. And yet love is the oldest force in the world. Did anyone ever hear of Eros having a father and mother? "First chaos, then the earth and then Eros." But perhaps that is not so significant. The important thing is what Eros means for us human beings. Eros alone – *Pause, vigorous gesticulation as Phaedrus casts around looking for words* – it is difficult to find the right expression – he alone, Eros – only he is able to make us feel shame. I mean that we feel ashamed doing wrong, something unfair, low, dishonorable. To be cowardly, for example. You only feel shame if you love. A person who does not love also does not do what is right. – And no one has ever seen that and said it! – Only the lover cares nothing about dying – for the beloved. Take the case of Alcestis – it was clearly easy for her to go to her death for the man she loved and had just married, in place of him. By contrast, this weakling, this lute-player Orpheus! He didn't have the courage to die. He wanted to steal down to Hades alive. And it was also in vain! – Being loved is not what matters most. This is exactly what is meant by the old saying: "The lover is more divine than the beloved. God dwells in him." Yes, that's what I wanted to say. – Man is worth nothing if he does not love. Love also makes him happy. Not only in life but also in death...

It seems as if something important is yet to come; but then Phaedrus, after making one or two attempts to speak, suddenly passes the figure on, putting it energetically in front of Pausanias.

The reaction to Phaedrus's speech is varied. Aristodemus is visibly very taken with it; he looks over to Socrates for confirmation. Socrates does not look at him but nods pensively, to himself. Aristophanes claps his hands and then drinks Phaedrus's health. Eryximachus follows suit, with some hesitation. Pausanias makes some skeptical gestures and then begins to speak.

He speaks with a kind of non-committal casualness, and in contrast to Phaedrus, without any real engagement. His words carry the stigma of implausibility. Despite all his skill in looking at things from the most varied points of view he is clearly not concerned with clarifying and throwing light on the subject.

PAUSANIAS *in a high-pitched voice, speaking with artificial ease*: I don't know, Phaedrus, whether it was so appropriate to handle the subject with ... with so little differentiation. Praising Eros so straightforwardly. As if there was only one Eros – which is simply not true! Certainly not here in Athens, where things are very, very colorful. And that's what's so good about it, I feel.

Here lovers are given every freedom. Or so it seems, as long as one keeps to what is in fact …well, the practice.

Aristophanes shows, quite openly, his fundamental mistrust of and displeasure at anything that Pausanias might say; he looks around in boredom and plays with his tobacco pouch. Pausanias notices that also in other respects he is not "getting through," and starts afresh after a pause.

In general, it is like this: when someone does something, no matter what it is, it is "in itself" neither good nor bad. For example, what we are doing here: talking, drinking, listening to music – none of that is "in itself" good and right.

Aristophanes impatiently grabs his full glass and drains it in one swallow.

What matters is how it is done. It has to – *hesitation; then a gesture meant to indicate "elegance"* – it has to be done with charm, with taste, grace, elegance – and then it is good and right! Otherwise not; otherwise it is low, repulsive, disgusting, embarrassing. And it is exactly the same with love. Anyone who has nothing further in mind than to get what he wants – brutally, without style or cultivation, acting clumsily and directly – *a negative, dismissive gesture.*

There are also two Aphrodites, one ordinary and another one which is normally called the "divine."

What follows is done in the manner of a carefully developed argument. Aristophanes listens to the next sentences in a way that shows he thinks it is all over the top. As we know, the divine Aphrodite has no mother. The feminine element is completely missing here. She has her origin purely in the male. Everyone knows the myth. There are simply no women in it. And I ask myself whether that could be the reason, one of the reasons, why the really ideal, the superior form of love ... is love of boys.

The last word has hardly been spoken when Aristophanes bangs his hand on the arm of his chair and breaks out into peals of laughter. He then starts to cough as if he had swallowed the wrong way.

Eryximachus attends to him. Pausanias, although insulted and looking on in astonishment, decides to put a good face on it, especially as Aristophanes apologizes between two fits of coughing.

ARISTOPHANES: Excuse me, I'm sorry. Naturally, I didn't mean to interrupt you.

PAUSANIAS: Oh, there's nothing to be sorry about. Why? No, nothing. Besides – with a slight bow to Phaedrus – I have finished anyway; what one says impromptu ... you know? *He shrugs and tries to trivialize what he has said while at the same time recommending that they think about it.*

Phaedrus now places the figure in front of Aristophanes, who is next to speak. But on top of everything else Aristophanes has now developed hiccups which with some effort he tries to suppress. He answers Phaedrus's invitation positively but with regret. Then he turns to Eryximachus, clearing his throat noisily and a couple of times interrupted by the hiccups which, as he is aware, are beginning to make him look ridiculous.

ARISTOPHANES: That's your job, Eryximachus. You

have to cure me of these ridiculous hiccups. Or you have to take my turn in speaking.

ERYXIMACHUS *a bit pompously*: I shall do both. *Turning to Phaedrus:* So, I am the next speaker?
Phaedrus nods in agreement and places the figure in front of Eryximachus.
And now for your hiccups. There are several methods. Hold your breath. No, that won't do it now. You'll have to gargle, with water!
Aristophanes stands up and goes towards the atrium; at a sign from Agathon a servant accompanies him. While he is still on the way, Eryximachus, who is right in his element, calls out another remedy.
If it is really persistent, put something up your nose to tickle it. Then sneeze! That works without fail.
Eryximachus now switches focus rather ceremoniously, moves the figure and places it exactly in front of him and while doing so throws his eye rapidly several times in the direction of the atrium as if he had only now discovered the right remedy. Gradually he composes himself and begins. He speaks with the didactic assurance of a knowledgeable sectarian who has found the universal formula which is valid for every aspect of reality and completely clears up the mysteries of the world and of life. Pausanias listens with interest and, for the most part, with approval. Phaedrus shows through his gestures and body language, which remain just within the borders of the acceptable, that all of this is not worth discussing. From time to time Socrates indicates ironically to Aristodemus his admiration for this perfect wielding of knowledge. Aristophanes, who only reappears for the second half of the speech, shows clearly that he, likewise, is not engaging with it. In Agathon's reaction genuine agreement is accompanied by the politeness of the host, which is everywhere manifested.

ERYXIMACHUS: To distinguish between two forms of Eros, as Pausanias suggests – well, I think one can approach the subject that way, no doubt. Although … I must say at the outset what medical science has taught me: that Eros is to be found everywhere, not just in the human sphere! Eros is everywhere! In everything: in animals, in plants that grow out of the earth. In the course of the stars, in the change of the seasons, in the relationship between the gods and men – Eros is at work everywhere. And it is always a question of controlling the forces of Eros: in astronomy, in the science of agriculture, in the function of priests. With regard to music, it is clear to everyone: harmony and rhythm – both are expressions of love. *The next sentence, although clearly said as an aside, is a specialty of Eryximachus: Heraclitus has misunderstood everything.* That is surely what Heraclitus meant. What he said has become famous, very famous. "Opposing elements come together as in a drawn bow" – well, that is, of course, not the way to express it. As long as something stands in opposition it can't be in accord! But let's move on.

Eryximachus pauses for a deep breath and "comes to the main point." Aristophanes has meantime returned to the group; at first he does not sit down but listens with interest to Eryximachus who, caught up in his speech, has not noticed him.

Naturally the science of healing, medicine, is completely controlled by the god Eros. It is nothing but the science of the love impulses in the human body. It is possible for them, at first, to be at odds with one another – *turning to Pausanias* – yes, a double Eros. So – where was I? Oh, yes. These movements of love can desire opposite things: cold and hot, bitter or sweet, dry or damp – and so on. Precisely this is what the master of medicine has to focus on. He has to bring it about that the warring forces unite in love; that they love one another. *At this point he notices Aristophanes.* Ah, Aristophanes, you are back! Yes, that's more or less the way I see it. Naturally, there is a lot more to be said. But you will speak about something quite different, won't you? You are cured, aren't you, and there is no hindrance? True? *He pushes the figure back in front of Aristophanes, who laughs and sits down.*

ARISTOPHANES: Yes, I am cured. But I was very surprised to hear how "the true Eros in the body," as you have just put it, can love such noise! First of all, this gargling, and then, when this didn't help, this, this ... racket! On the other hand, it is true, I "love" sneezing from time to time.

ERYXIMACHUS: Be careful! That's dangerous. To be laughing at me just when you want to begin speaking. You could have had peace to make your speech. But now you are even compelling me to be critical, very critical, and to keep an eye on you – in case what you say is comical.

ARISTOPHANES *interrupts him*: Oh, comical is allowed. That's part of my trade. As long as it's not laughable. *Aristophanes drinks a mighty draught of wine. Then he leans back in his armchair, becomes very pensive for a few moments, and begins. Sometimes the tone of his speech changes unexpectedly; religious seriousness, though not expressed with pathos, switches in a flash to comic burlesque – which, however, does not relativize the seriousness but, instead, deepens it. The listeners, who may have been expecting something merely witty, are not sure how to react. Phaedrus feels confirmed in his view and agrees. Socrates is benignly pensive. Aristodemus is, as a young man, especially taken by the burlesque interplay. Pausanias and Eryximachus are somewhat disconcerted; they feel that they misunderstood and that their superior standpoint is being questioned. Agathon shows non-committal respect.*

ARISTOPHANES *first turning to Eryximachus*: Yes, it's true, Eryximachus. I do intend to say something quite different from what you have said. And the same applies to you, Pausanias. I agree with Phaedrus. *A look of agreement in the direction of Phaedrus.* People haven't at all understood the power of Eros. For that it is first of all necessary to understand human nature. We have, above all, to consider what has happened to it. Our nature was not, in time immemorial, the same as it is now; it used to be quite different. Formerly, in the beginning, the human shape was round, like a globe; it was perfect. Like the heavenly bodies, the sun and the moon.
The following sentence is spoken, casually, to Aristodemus. If someone was in a hurry he did a cartwheel – he could do that effortlessly – and so moved off quickly, supported, of course, by four arms and four legs. *Aristophanes empties his glass with one mighty swallow. The glass is immediately filled again. He now becomes completely serious again.* But man was not only perfect in the external shape of his body. He also had his head full of great thoughts. Homer described it: he tried to find his way into the heavens to do battle with the gods. But the gods consulted about how they could

punish human beings. And Zeus said: I will take away their excessive strength; I will cut them into two halves. *Speaking to Aristodemus and gesticulating wildly:* That's exactly what happened: with one blow human beings were cut in half – just the same as one cuts up pears to conserve them, or an egg, using a horse hair. *After a pause, as if speaking to himself:* Yes, every one of us is incomplete; we are only a piece of a human being. And everyone is full of the desire to regain this original round perfection. – That is the ultimate explanation – of love! Pleasure is not the reason why lovers so passionately desire to be with one another. It is something quite different. The soul, of course, is not able to put a name on it. The soul only senses it and entertains mysteries about it. If Hephaistos, the divine blacksmith, were to come to them as they lay together and, hammer in hand, ask them what they really wanted from one another, they wouldn't know what answer to give him. It is that we want to be intact and rounded, whereas we are now, through wrongdoing, incomplete and divided. What do we want, fundamentally? We want to be intact and whole! As we were once upon a time. As in the beginning. And the quest for that – that is exactly what love is, nothing else. That is what Eros is. Only that!

Aristophanes, in conclusion, has banged the table with the palm of his hand. What follows is spoken first to Aristodemus and then, with gestures of confirmation and emphasis, to Phaedrus.

So, what follows from all of that? We must honor the gods! Otherwise we may well be divided again and then hop around on one leg as dancers do on a wineskin in peasants' games.

Above all, Eros deserves, in every way, to be praised and celebrated in song – because he gives us such hope: namely, the healing of our being and bliss.

After he has emptied his glass, Aristophanes, looking around the circle, passes the figure on to Agathon.

Oh, only two more, Agathon and Socrates? *Then to Eryximachus:* Now, what about your criticism? What do you think? Was what I said really comical? Or ludicrous?

Eryximachus has become somewhat uneasy and is visibly attempting to avoid making any objective response.

ERYXIMACHUS: Oh no, not at all. Anyway, I don't think that Agathon and Socrates will be at a loss for something to say – not at all, despite the extent of your contribution. They are both very experienced people. So I am quite happy.

SOCRATES *to Eryximachus:* It's all right for you! You've made your speech. If you were in my place, if you were where I will soon be after Agathon has also spoken – you would be very worried, just as I am.

Agathon turns to Socrates, somewhat in the manner of the star who is used to success.

AGATHON: Don't say, Socrates, that anyone expects wonders from me. You are making me embarrassed; you are trying to put a jinx on me.

SOCRATES: Oh, I must have a bad memory – after I have just witnessed how assured you were coming onto the stage with the actors. You were not the slightest bit shy as you looked at the thousands of people.

AGATHON: The thousands! Do you really think that my head was so full of theatre that I didn't know: a thousand philistines are less to be feared than a handful of clever people?

SOCRATES: No, that's not what I mean, of course. That would not be very nice of me. Besides, we few were also amongst the thousands …
Agathon shakes his head vigorously and wants to put something right. But Socrates raises his hand energetically and does not let him speak.
Fine. I know that in the company of wise people, whoever they might be, you would be ashamed to do anything bad.

AGATHON *interrupts him*: That's exactly what I wanted to say.

SOCRATES *cunningly springing the trap*: Yes, and in the company of the many, the "thousands," would you not be ashamed?
Agathon has become uneasy; he stands up in agitation and tries to explain more precisely. Phaedrus picks up the figure and places it energetically on the table in front of Agathon.

PHAEDRUS: If you answer him now it won't matter in the least to Socrates what happens to the rest of us here – once he has found someone he can debate with. But first of all I now have to call in the speeches in honor of Eros. And that's what I'll do. You can have your debate afterwards.
Agathon sits down, visibly relieved, takes up the figure as if he enjoyed touching it; then, with a smile, puts it down again on the table, turning it to face him.

AGATHON: Excellent, Phaedrus! Of course, there is nothing to stop me from beginning. I can converse with Socrates often enough at a later time. All right.

The Eros speech that follows is not without a tinge of narcissism. Agathon praises what he would like to be himself or what he thinks he already is. Furthermore, he is clearly speaking with a "literary" aim. He is concerned with form: the speech is to be taken as "poiema," as a verbal work of art, whereby the speaker knows only too well that one does not make a show of such qualities. – The listeners are visibly inclined to concede the host and prize-winner considerable status. Pausanias, above all, shows his uncritical enthusiasm right from the beginning. Aristophanes does not hold back with his discreet irony, both in his gestures and in his body language. Socrates listens intently, but his face is inscrutable.

AGATHON: A eulogy, I think – in every eulogy the speaker must begin by talking about the person to be eulogized, not about what he does or what impression he makes. This is the error that all the previous speakers have committed. They have spoken less about Eros than about human beings and about the gifts they owe to Eros. I, therefore, shall speak about Eros himself. – And to begin with, I will say he is blissful. Although, of course, all gods are blissful – but he is the happiest of them all. Why? Because he is the most beautiful – and this again because he is the youngest. Phaedrus, I agree with you on many counts, but not in this. Eros is not the oldest! From the depths of his heart he hates old age. He flees from the old and stays with the young. These primeval acts of violence in the stories about the gods: castration, imprisonment in chains and all the rest of those frightful things – it would not have happened if Eros had already been there. Roughness, cruelty are foreign to him like everything – well, how should I say? – like everything that is "not tender." It hurts his vulnerable sensibility. It is not his thing to offer resistance. He snuggles up, he is like flowing water. He has the tenderness of a flower. And wherever something blooms and gives off its scent – that is where he settles, the most beautiful one.

PAUSANIAS *claps his hands in applause*: Superb!
The others impatiently make signs to him not to interrupt Agathon. Phaedrus makes a move to pick up the figure and demonstratively put it down again in front of Agathon.

AGATHON: But Eros is not only handsome, he is also good! – What, then, does justice mean? That a person gets what is his. Now, everyone serves Eros of his own free will – and so no wrong is done to anyone (by Eros). What are self-control and moderation? That one keeps pleasure and desire in check. But Eros is stronger than all of them; he controls them all, without exception.
And bravery? Who was the victor in the battle between Ares and Eros? Not the god of war, but Eros! – And finally, with regard to wisdom – Eryximachus, you have spoken about your particular discipline, the art of healing; I must now speak about mine, about poetry. Is it not Eros who makes poets? But it is the same with all of the arts. Brilliance only comes through Eros. Anyone not touched by him does not shine and remains in darkness.
What, then, are the gifts of Eros? I will try to say it in my own way, in verse:
Peace amongst men,
Brightly mirroring sea,
Calm magically stormless,
Deep sleep far from pain.

Strangeness vanishes,
Belonging appears,
Wildness is banished,
Mildness remains!
Eros, who favors the good,
Observed by the wise,
Beloved of the gods –
He sings this hymn
And charms the hearts of gods and men;
And all beings join in
With shouts of joy.

All clap their hands in applause that is mingled with enthusiastic exclamations: Wonderful! Masterly! Glorious! *Agathon receives all of this without showing too obviously how much he enjoys the success. Then he concludes with an elegant and relaxed bow to Phaedrus like a gestural quotation from a courtly play:*
So, Phaedrus, that is my speech – a bit on the playful side, but, I hope, not lacking in seriousness.
Again there is loud applause but through it the voice of Socrates can be heard as he turns to Eryximachus.

SOCRATES: Now, noble friend, what do you think? Have I not every reason to be afraid? Was my prophecy not fulfilled? I am completely at a loss!

ERYXIMACHUS: The prophecy that Agathon's speech would be excellent, yes. But you at a loss? Let someone else believe that.

SOCRATES: You and your blissful innocence! Am I to open my mouth after such a speech? No, impossible. Above all, this incredible conclusion. There's not the slightest possibility that I could produce something as fine as that. And I would have wanted to run away in embarrassment if I had known where to go.

After a pause, turning to all in a different, more serious tone: I must say that this has become completely clear to me: I should never have agreed to participate, never decided to speak in such company. I am only making a show of myself. And yet I did say I understood things concerning Eros! That may be. But how to eulogize something – I have no idea how to do that. How simple-minded it is to think that in praising something you just have to tell the truth about it, no matter what. But as I see it now, that is not what is required. You gather as much fine material as you can find and heap it onto the person to be eulogized. If it is not all quite true there is no harm done. But I cannot praise Eros in this way. Nor do I want to. So, what do I do now, Phaedrus? Can you accept a speech about Eros which attempts to say what is true?

The listeners are clearly somewhat disconcerted; there are signs of agitation. Pausanias is visibly outraged and claps silently, ostentatiously showing his support for Agathon, whose sensitivity to criticism he knows.

Phaedrus, as he places the figure in front of Socrates, says with undaunted firmness:

PHAEDRUS: Socrates, speak exactly as you think you must.

SOCRATES *pushing the figure a little to one side*: Good, Phaedrus, thank you. But first, before I begin you must permit me to ask Agathon a few small questions – only tiny things.

Phaedrus agrees to this with an exaggeratedly theatrical gesture in a show of his importance.

So, Agathon, I found what you said at the beginning very good: first one should speak about Eros himself. But this is where my first question is going. – Eros, love therefore, is surely always directed and related to something or somebody. Just as when I say: "brother" or "father" – it is always the brother of someone and the father of a son or daughter. Agreed?
Agathon nods in friendly curiosity, wondering where this is heading.

SOCRATES: Good. But isn't it the same with love? Isn't it necessarily the love of something – I mean for something?

AGATHON *bewildered*: Of course, what else?

SOCRATES *insistent and inscrutable*: Good! Please hang onto that. Next, this: does not love long for what it loves?

AGATHON *still at a loss*: Yes!

SOCRATES *slyly narrowing his eyes to slits, not looking at Agathon but at Aristophanes and Phaedrus*: Does love long for what it already possesses? Or does it not yet have it?

AGATHON *hesitantly*: It looks as if it does not yet possess it.

SOCRATES: More precisely, please, Agathon. Does it merely "look as if," or is it the case? Must it not be so? If a person longs for something, he needs the thing he longs for: the fact is he does not have it! And where something is not needed it is not longed for. In my opinion, anyway, it cannot be otherwise. Do you not agree?

AGATHON: I do!

SOCRATES: Good. Of course, a person who, let us say, already has health can want health; but that means in this case, that he would like to have it also in the future. – Should I sum up what we have said so far? Love is love for something, and indeed for something which one does not already possess. *He looks around the group.*

AGATHON *after some hesitation*: Yes.

SOCRATES: Now remember what you have said about Eros. To what does he direct himself?
Agathon remains silent, slightly stubborn.
Didn't you say beauty?

AGATHON: Yes, that's what I said.

SOCRATES: And of course you are right. But ... we have agreed that love longs for something that it does not already have?
Agathon shrugs his shoulders but then is forced to agree.
And so Eros needs beauty; but he does not possess it. That's exactly what he does not have.
Basically Agathon surrenders; but he would like to save the situation and himself by striking a non-committal, sociable note, and he answers with a somewhat forced laugh:

AGATHON: It is possible that I understand nothing of what I was talking about earlier. Perhaps it is as you say. Nothing else occurs to me.
Now, with a gesture which says the topic has been exhausted, he puts down his weapons: I'm not the man to contradict you. That's all.

SOCRATES: Well, you can't contradict the truth! But

contradicting Socrates is not difficult. But, all right, I'll let you off the hook.

During the first sentences of the speech that follows Socrates shifts the figure from one hand into the other and puts it on the table, as if playfully at first, at two different places alternately, one of which is to designate his own place and the other that of Diotima. Socrates speaks in three different roles: as reporter, as partner in conversation with Diotima, and as Diotima herself. In the first case he mostly takes the figure from the table and holds it in his hand, while, in the direct delivery of the conversation, he indicates through the alternating placement of the figure on the table which of the two is now speaking. But he does not carry it through very exactly. With a good-humored respectful bow to Phaedrus he starts again with some hesitation:

And so now I shall try ...

Aristodemus interrupts him after listening to the conversation with Agathon with tense enthusiasm but also impatience, and now looks triumphantly around the circle.

ARISTODEMUS: At last Socrates himself is going to speak!

SOCRATES: I'm afraid I am going to disappoint you, dear fellow. No, strictly speaking it won't be "my" speech.

ARISTODEMUS: Then whose?

SOCRATES: I am going to repeat what was once said to me by someone else; at least I will, as far as my memory serves me. This other person is a woman, Diotima, priestess from Mantinea, the city of oracles. She instructed me on this subject a long time ago. She was extremely wise in these things – and in many other things besides. I had said to Diotima much the same, my dear Agathon, as you have said in your speech: Eros, a great god, the quintessence of beauty – and so forth. But Diotima proved me wrong – and with the arguments with which you are now familiar. I, too, said at that time: "But is not the whole world in agreement that Eros is a great divinity?" – "The whole world?" she said. "Do you mean all those who have no knowledge, or also those who do have knowledge?" – "I mean simply: all!" "And how does it stand with those who do not consider him a god at all?" – "Who could that be?" "For example: you! And I!" – Naturally I did not understand a word of what she was saying. But she just laughed at me. "You think all the gods, all without exception, are happy and beautiful and good – or don't you?" "Of course!" "But Eros – don't you agree that he is only longing for happiness and beauty, but does not already possess them?" "Yes, I agree." "Then don't you agree that you don't consider him to be a god." "But what is he then?" – "He is a great daimon, Socrates, situated in the middle between the mortals and the immortals. He is one of those who keep the conversation between gods and men going." And she added: "Anyone who understands this is daimonic; by comparison, all other knowledge and understanding is philistinism. But what you said, Socrates, especially about beauty, that Eros is beautiful and even the quintessence of beauty – that does not surprise me so very much. You thought, namely, that Eros was the beloved, whereas he is in fact the lover! What is loved is beautiful, perfect and blissful. The ones who love, the lovers – they are quite different!" "Well, if that's how it stands with Eros what good is he to us?" Diotima answered me with great patience and started from a long way back: "Eros, as we have said, loves the beautiful and the good."

Here Socrates pauses and looks at Aristophanes, who is filling his pipe but now stops and braces himself for a battle.

Anyway, Aristophanes, with the help of Diotima I realized this: when we truly love we don't look for the half that belongs to us. Nor the wholeness we have lost – unless ...

ARISTOPHANES *interrupts him in an intense state of agitation, in which he puts down his pipe and whatever else he was holding*:
The whole is perfection, and perfection is ...

SOCRATES *undeterred, finishes the sentence he has begun*: ... unless this whole were itself to be the good. For that alone is what we really love. And for its sake we would, if necessary, do without wholeness.

ARISTOPHANES: Phaedrus, here I must ...

PHAEDRUS *interrupting him in a firm but friendly tone*: First Socrates has to finish his speech. He has the floor.

SOCRATES *again places the figure emphatically in the place he pretends is for Diotima and continues, speaking with clearly intentional calmness*: "So, when Eros" – Diotima said –, "loves the beautiful and the good, what does he want?" – "To get them," I said, "the beautiful and the good!" – "And what happens to the person who gets them?" – "Happiness." – "That's right. The happy are happy by virtue of having what is good for them. And there is no need to ask further. Why do you want to be happy? – You don't ask that. – But happiness is not happiness if it does not last. And it can't be

otherwise. Love needs unlimited duration, it wants
immortality, it wants eternity. It doesn't merely have
beauty in its sights, but reproduction. Its aim is not
just the flower, but the lasting fruit.

*Socrates, who has said the last things largely to himself,
looks pensively for a time at young Aristodemus, who has
been listening to him full of enthusiasm. There is a slight
interruption due to the replenishing of the glasses. Eryximachus has another bunch of grapes brought to him and begins to eat them rapturously. Then Socrates resumes.*

This and much more Diotima said to me at that time.
Naturally, I haven't understood it all, and some of it I
may have forgotten. She was saving up the most as-
tonishing part. It is something I remember very exactly. It was like an initiation into the mysteries. That's
what she called it herself. And she was in some doubt
about whether I was quite mature enough for "the ultimate vision," as she called it. "In any case, try to follow me as far as you can." What she now said about
the gradation of the forms of Eros – and that even the
lowest rung, the sensual tremor caused by the body's
physical beauty, could be a step on the way, a rung on
the ladder of ascent – all of this was totally new to me
and amazing. And I was no longer even able to ask a
question.

A rung on the ladder, said Diotima, is not only to be
stood on but left behind, otherwise there is no ascent.
About the last, highest rung, which strictly speaking is
no longer a rung [it is the peak to which the rungs lead]
– of this ultimate form of Eros Diotima said the following: "A person who, in matters of love, truly reaches the
goal will suddenly, unexpectedly, behold something
wonderful: that which is beautiful of itself, that 'is'

eternal, that neither becomes nor passes away, neither waxes nor wanes; not: beautiful here, here not beautiful; not: now yes, now no; not: beautiful for some, for others not beautiful. It is also not beautiful the way a face or a hand or a piece of jewelry or a dress or any other tangible thing is beautiful. It is not beauty 'in' anything else, whether in a living being or the earth or the sky.

It is and consists in itself, eternal und unchangeable. And now life– so said Diotima –now life is, if ever at all, truly worth living since one sees the divine and the beautiful. Now one experiences being a beloved of god and being beyond death."

Aristodemus is the first to applaud. The others also are friendly in their applause. Socrates quickly ends it. He says, dismissively:

So this, Phaedrus, and you others, is what Diotima said. And, as for me, I believed her. Nothing in the world can be more helpful to human nature in reaching that goal than Eros. Therefore everyone should honor him as I do myself. *Turning to Phaedrus:* Can you let that pass as a eulogy? If not, give it another name – whichever you like.

Phaedrus vigorously fends off this suggestion. His gestures indicate his approval. During the last sentences there has been a repeated knocking on the house door. Agathon beckons to a servant.

AGATHON: Go and see who that is. But only let him in if we know him. Clear?

The servant goes out through the atrium, from where soon the voice of a slightly tipsy Alcibiades can be heard. He is asking for Agathon in a loud voice. – Aristophanes makes another attempt to present his argument but is then immediately interrupted by Alcibiades.

ARISTOPHANES *to Socrates, very quickly and impatiently*: Love, you say, is not in such of totality? To my mind, Socrates, it is simply a question of how you define it. The whole, what belongs to us, what is good for us ... *Suddenly the listeners' attention is diverted; it is, so to speak, sucked away by Alcibiades, who enters from the atrium. At the same moment the music strikes up again; it will continue right to the end. At first, Alcibiades remains standing at the entrance. Agathon has stood up and, with a smile, looks over to him expectantly. Alcibiades has two enormous chrysanthemums in the buttonhole of his jacket which he now, with effort and circumstance, tries to pull out. This preoccupies him so much that he is scarcely able to look up.*

ALCIBIADES: Where's Agathon? I'm looking for Agathon! I have to decorate him. I have to congratulate the victor.

AGATHON *goes over towards him*: Here I am Alcibiades. Come in. You are very welcome here.

ALCIBIADES *still fiddling with the flowers*: Really? Do you allow a drunk to take part in your festivities? Yesterday, as you know, I simply wasn't able to come. It just wasn't on. So. Here, wear these flowers, lucky man! *In the meantime Agathon, laughing, has brought him to the bench on which he himself was sitting with Socrates. Socrates moves up a little.*
Come and sit down. At my right hand. There is room enough here for three.

ALCIBIADES *who, while he is sitting down, is still trying to put the flowers on Agathon and has therefore not really taken cognizance of Socrates or anyone else*: For three, you said? Then who's the third? *He turns to Socrates and recognizes him. He immediately jumps up again, puts his hands to his head in an exaggerated theatrical gesture, covering his eyes – and so forth.*

Good God! Socrates! It's you! Have you been lying in wait again? You are always suddenly there where I least expect you.

SOCRATES *pretending to be intimidated, to Agathon*: If he becomes violent you will have to help me. I'm afraid of this madman. Or, better still, try to placate him for me.

ALCIBIADES: No. No talk of placating. We'll settle our account another time. Certainly not now. Now, Agathon, give one of the flowers back to me. *He takes it himself and fixes it on Socrates.* I must decorate this wonderful man as well – because he is always the victor. Over everyone!

He then sits down, rather wearily, between Socrates and Agathon, and for the first time looks around at the group. He extends his arms in a welcoming gesture.

ALCIBIADES: Greetings, everyone. But you are not drinking; you are completely sober! That's not right; that is against tradition. Therefore I shall appoint for you, until you have drunk enough, a master of the symposium: myself!

He picks up the small glass that had been put in front of him and looks at it contemptuously.

Agathon, don't you have a large vessel to drink from? No, fill up that bowl for me; then we can pass it around and all drink from it.

He points to a vase-shaped vessel on the side-board. A servant, hesitant and smiling, goes to fetch it.

Eryximachus, holding a few of the grapes in his hand, has from the very beginning reacted to Alcibiades's behavior with displeasure. He now interrupts him:

ERYXIMACHUS: Stop, stop, stop! Alcibiades, do we really want to do that? Simply pour wine into ourselves?

ALCIBIADES: Ah, Eryximachus, son of the most sober father there ever was, greetings!

ERYXIMACHUS *raising his hand somewhat frostily but not without friendliness*: Greetings to you too. But now tell us, how are we to do this?

ALCIBIADES *having immediately forgotten his proposal*: What do you suggest? You tell us how to proceed. A man of medical science has more weight than many others put together.

ERYXIMACHUS: Listen. Long before you arrived we decided that each of us in turn should deliver a eulogy to Eros. And that's what we have done. Everyone has spoken. Now it would be your turn.

ALCIBIADES: That's all very fine. But a drunk in competition with non-drunks? That wouldn't be fair. Besides, in the presence of Socrates I would never dare to praise anyone else, not even a god. He would kill me!

SOCRATES *speaking to him in a calm and friendly tone*: Don't be so blasphemous!

ERYXIMACHUS: All right then, if you like, make a eulogy to Socrates!

ALCIBIADES *who suddenly likes this suggestion*: Are you serious? I can get my revenge on him in front of you all?

SOCRATES: What do you intend to do? Do you want to make fun of me?

ALCIBIADES: I want to tell the truth. Or do you not allow that?

SOCRATES: Not only allow it, I even demand it.

ALCIBIADES: Fine! As soon as I say something that is not true you will interrupt me. But you mustn't be surprised if I dredge up from my memory now this, now that, as it is occurs to me. In my condition it is not so easy to describe your wondrousness in the organized form it deserves.

The speech that follows is a series of thoughts which appear strung together without any inner cohesion. Each time something is narrated a short pause ensues in which Alcibiades empties his glass or lights a cigarette; and then suddenly the next thought follows. The group, now generally taking to the wine in greater measure, is in good spirits. There is much laughter. Socrates, too, is in very good form. Sometimes he does certainly become very serious and seems to be thinking of something else.

Aristodemus, although intensely interested, is struggling to stay awake.

ALCIBIADES: Let me begin to speak in praise of Socrates. Every now and then a comparison occurs to me, a similarity. *Turning around to Socrates:* Don't see it as mockery; no, it is the truth! – I am saying, therefore, that Socrates is like one of these figures that can be opened up – the ones you see in wood-carvers' shops. There you have a figure squatting down like Silenus and playing a shepherd's pipe. But inside: the image of a god! Does he not look like a satyr?

Socrates makes a dismissive gesture. Alcibiades does not leave him room to speak.

You can't deny it. But aren't you also a flute-player? A superb, inspiring one? Except that you charm us without an instrument, just with your words. When we hear another speaker, no matter how famous, we say he has spoken well, even outstandingly – "fantastically." But deep down we are unmoved; it means nothing to us. But when you speak, you speak to the heart. You must all think I am completely drunk but I'll say it anyway: when I hear his words my heart begins to pound and I feel the tears are coming. It is a kind of subjugation. I have often thought I simply cannot keep on living – not the way I do. *To Socrates:* Will you say that is not true?

And today, now, in this very moment – I am sure: if I were to listen to him I could not resist him. He compels you; you have to confess to yourself: you are not as you should be. And so I have blocked my ears as if to the song of the sirens. I have run away – otherwise I would sit at his feet all my life.

You all know it is not like me to feel ashamed in anyone's presence. I know I don't manage to contradict him to his face and to say, for instance: Why *must* I do what you say? And so I run away looking for public applause. Sometimes I would wish there was no Socrates anymore. But that would be even worse for me. So I simply don't know what to do with this man. Don't be deceived! None of you knows him. For example, you see Socrates playing the lover, ecstatic, enthused, naive. But that is only his Silenus-like exterior! That is Silenus! He is only playing games with all of us. Wealth, youth, beauty – all of that simply means nothing to him!

I don't know if anyone else has seen this inward divine image hidden in this Silenus. In any case, I have been able to see it. I still feel the sharp pain, the shaming, this boundless mocking. It was worse than the bite of a viper. An angry bite into the middle of your heart or soul – whichever you like to call it. And yet I could do nothing about it: I had to admire this man. I have never yet met anyone like him.

At that time I was still very young. Later we were on military campaigns together. The hardship seemed to mean nothing to him. If there was nothing to eat and all the others were moaning, he didn't. But in drinking, if prevailed upon to drink, he could outlast everybody. And yet, unbelievably, no one ever saw him drunk.

But now listen to this: one morning he was standing, deep in thought, on the one spot; something or other had occurred to him. Probably you are familiar with that.

General laughter. Oh yes. *Agathon finds this too obvious reference to the evening somewhat embarrassing. Over Alcibiades's head he shares a cheerful, understanding look with Socrates, who, for his part, continues with his superior smile.*

But this was on a military camp. Meantime it had become midday. The soldiers noticed him, and one brought it to the attention of the other. But Socrates remained standing there pondering. In the evening, after the meal – it was summer time and the nights were hot – some of them brought their blankets out of the tents and lay down in the open air. They wanted to see whether he would also stand there throughout the night. And, in fact, he didn't leave until sunrise!

And in the battle, or rather in the retreat at Delion, the army was in disarray and was scattered and pouring back – I saw Socrates, well, I can only say, "going on his way" exactly as you have described it, Aristophanes, "striding along like a Marabou stork, casting his eye in all directions," calmly fixing friend and foe with his gaze; but there was no doubt: this man would strike back hard if anyone bothered him.

Clearly, there is no one to compare with him. No human being, anyway. Pericles, Achilles – they can be compared with someone. Socrates cannot. At the most, with a satyr and Silenus.

Pausanias, who has been wandering around for a while, has discovered on the sideboard just such an openable figure of Silenus. He opens and closes it a couple of times and then places it opened on the table. Alcibiades picks it up and continues, handing the figure to Phaedrus.

His speeches, too – I forgot to say – they, too, are like the Silenus figures. They have to be opened! At first sight they seem to be spoken in jest. He speaks about cobblers and blacksmiths and pack mules. And it always seems to be the same thing. And the unsuspecting listener laughs. But if one knows how to open these speeches one sees that, amongst all the other things that are being said, these speeches alone make sense. They are completely divine.

So, friends, that is what I have to say in praise of this man. But I did not want to omit what I have to say against him. You should be warned, Agathon. Don't be deceived by him. Don't be wise when it's too late!

Laughter, applause, cheers. Eryximachus has stood up and obviously intends to take his leave. As Socrates begins his reply, he turns around again and listens. Aristodemus swaps his stool with the armchair that Eryximachus has just vacated. He puts his feet up on the stool. He is unable to stay awake a minute longer. Gradually Socrates's words, as well as the laughter they evoke, and Alcibiades's protests begin to fade. Everything seems to be coming from far away, then it is suddenly close by, and finally it is completely inaudible.

SOCRATES *with a knowing, sly look on his face*: So drunk, dear friend, you surely are not. Otherwise you would not have managed so cleverly to obscure the real aim of your speech – until, at the very end, it became apparent: namely, that you had nothing else in mind than to separate us, Agathon and me. But I can see through you.

AGATHON: Yes, he immediately sat down between us!

ALCIBIADES: But didn't you put me in that place yourself?

SOCRATES: Your satyr and Silenus game has been unmasked.

AGATHON *changing his place*: Socrates, I'm sitting next to you.

SOCRATES *to Agathon*: Don't give him a chance!

ALCIBIADES: It's always the same with this man …
All of this is no longer clearly audible. It is lost in the music which favors [and also depicts] Aristodemus's sleep. Finally the voice of the speaker is heard again. The camera has now focused entirely on the fitfully sleeping Aristodemus, who continually tries to find the right position for sleeping.

SPEAKER: The narrator has become tired. He is no longer

listening. That is the reason why we, too, know nothing of what was then said during the night. The conversation continues until early morning. According to Aristodemus, he didn't wake up until after cock crow. Plato's "symposium" has, therefore, no conclusion. The point, so to speak, is lost. At least, that is how it seems. But appearances are deceptive. There is definitely an end and a result. It is merely that it is not apparent. But with Plato's dialogues that is almost the rule.

The camera, which has again begun to wander, shows a scene which in the meantime has completely changed.
Eryximachus and Phaedrus have gone. The servants are asleep on the stools. Near the door to the terrace Alcibiades and Pausanias put their heads together and from time to time burst out laughing. Aristodemus yawns uninhibitedly but is wide awake again and attentive. Socrates is sitting up straight in his earlier place and is speaking to Aristophanes and Agathon. Both strain to give him their attention but are still only half listening. Aristophanes is lying with his elbows resting on a bench, while Agathon, sitting next to Socrates, is leaning back in exhaustion with his head resting against the wall.
Socrates tries to lend emphasis to his words by energetic gestures and, in order to demonstrate the interchangeability of writers of tragedy and comedy, moves the figure back and forth between Agathon and Aristophanes. What he says remains, like everything else, inaudible.
[*Inaudible dialogue:*

SOCRATES: Dearest Aristophanes, you are not listening! But what I'm saying is for you. Agathon understood it long ago.

He picks up the figure and places it energetically in front of Aristophanes and then in front of Agathon.
This is the writer of comedy. But if that is what he really is then he is at the same time a writer of tragedy. If he is not both he is nothing.]

Socrates suddenly stands up, slaps Aristophanes on the shoulder in farewell and has Agathon show him out. Aristodemus follows.

SPEAKER *calmly continuing*: And so Aristodemus reports that he has heard – and seen – how Socrates, the only one not worn out, is still, early in the morning, trying to make one single thesis clear to both poets: namely, that only someone who can write a comedy is able also to write a tragedy and vice versa.
Herein lies the hidden point and the conclusion. This is not at all a new theme. Eros is still the subject, especially now. Has it not become amply clear that Eros is nothing less than the daimonic force of existence itself? The force which again and again casts us out of our comfort zone in the everyday world – something which is comic, or tragic, or both together?

While Socrates, at the door, turns around again to Agathon and to the spectators to take his leave, raising his hand in greeting, the music becomes louder and ends with a complex fugal grand finale.

THE DEATH OF SOCRATES

Written in memory of my son Thomas Pieper 6.21.1936-7.25.1964

Characters

SOCRATES

PHAEDO

ECHECRATES

CRITO

SIMMIAS

CEBES

APOLLODORUS

WARDEN

COURT BAILIFF

At the request of a visitor, an eyewitness narrates the conversa-
tions and events in the prison cell on the last day of Socrates's
life. This starting point of Plato's dialogue Phaedo is taken up
and carried through in what follows here. But in our play
Phaedo's report begins somewhat further back, in such a way
that Socrates's speech in his defense is included, as well as the
story included in Crito about the failed attempt to persuade him
to escape. The texts taken from the three dialogues which make
up by far the greatest part of the play, although substantially
abridged, correspond very accurately to the text of Plato's dia-
logues, whereas in the passages spoken by Phaedo a cautious
commentary is attempted.

The action takes place in an open area and in the prison. Both
scenes are to be thought of as being as unrelated as possible to
any particular time. There should be no realistic details associ-
ated with ancient Athens, nor should a particularly modern im-
pression be given.

The clothes should be what is now contemporary in style, but
not eye-catching and certainly not appearing particularly fash-
ionable.

The characters

SOCRATES, *seventy years old, but, as will be seen above all in*
the first part of the play, he has lost nothing of his love of
debate and irony. But this time the basic mood is one of
solemn seriousness, which, however, is countered by his su-
perior cheerfulness, and there is no pathos. – His clothing
in the first part is middle-class average, not particularly el-
egant. In the prison he is not dressed like a prisoner, but
there is no tie or collar.

PHAEDO, *one of the enthusiastic students around Socrates, is*
about twenty-five years old. Full of passion and impatience,

he is still deeply affected by the trial and condemnation of his beloved teacher, whose attitude he is only now slowly beginning to comprehend, despite all his admiration for Socrates. – As reporter he wears summer clothing, including a white sports shirt; as a visitor in the prison he wears a dark roll-neck pullover.

ECHÉCATES *is about fifty years old; a teacher type, educated, intellectually alert.*

CRITO *is about the same age as Socrates; a shrewd practical man, uncomplicated and straightforward.*

SIMMIAS AND CEBES, *both about thirty-five years old, friends with one another and with Socrates. Very interested in philosophical themes, but they are not intellectuals of the sophist kind. SIMMIAS: open, likeable, somewhat naïve. CEBES: a keen mind, grappling with problems.*

APOLLODORUS, *about thirty years old, a long-time follower of Socrates. Inclined to excess of feeling, he follows the course of events in the death cell silently but with obvious sympathy. [This figure could perhaps be omitted.]*

WARDEN: *corpulent, good natured, somewhat soft, easy to influence. His official position is identifiable only by his uniform – a not very imposing jacket with a row of shiny buttons. No headgear, nothing aggressive about him.*

COURT BAILIFF, *a faceless but not inhuman functionary. Military uniform; helmet and belt.*

An open space with trees. Bright summer's day.
Phaedo and Echecrates, in conversation, enter from the side and then sit down on a tree trunk [or a fallen pillar]. Phaedo has taken off his jacket which he lays down beside him. His narration is more a dramatic visualization than a pure

report. The more he is moved by his memory the more passionate his gestures become. The basic mood is angry admiration.

PHAEDO: No, no! I have time. I have time for this. You were right: naturally I was there. Well, no, not "naturally," not at all! Incredibly! Sometimes I can't believe that I, Phaedo from Elis, was really with him in the death cell, on his last day, almost the entire time, and that I saw with my very own eyes how he drank the cup of poison. – So I have to keep on speaking again and again about how all of it unfolded, one thing after the other. But you know the facts, too, don't you?

ECHECRATES: Yes, the first news came, in fact, very soon. But much of it seemed somewhat improbable. This strangely long time, for example, between the judgment and the – well, execution. Why was that?

PHAEDO: Well, that's a story in its own right. Every year there is a cult sailing across the sea from Athens to Delos, to the island of Apollo. An old custom. I don't know how many hundreds of years it has been happening.

ECHECRATES: I am aware of it. But what has it to do …

PHAEDO *interrupts him*: And while this festive mission is underway no one can be executed by the state.

ECHECRATES: The ship had only just sailed?

PHAEDO: It was even still in the harbor. But – exactly one day before the sentence was passed the priests had ceremonially decorated the prow of the ship. This the moment the sailing begins. That's the reason for the long time.

ECHECRATES: But then I'm wondering about something else. Is there nothing you could do? I mean, was he in strict confinement. Was it not possible to spirit him away? It wouldn't be the first time something like that had happened.

PHAEDO: Yes, yes, I know. But there's nothing we didn't try!

ECHECRATES: The most incomprehensible thing for us was the death sentence itself. That it could come to that. Socrates not able to defend himself! Or was he not permitted to speak? Was he ...

PHAEDO *interrupts him*: Of course he was allowed to speak. And he was in the best possible form.

ECHECRATES: But?

PHAEDO: Well – he didn't defend himself. From his very first word he spoke as if he expected to be condemned.

ECHECRATES: So, what happened? What did he say? Tell me. Presumably the charge was read out first of all.

PHAEDO: Yes, the charge was read out and the justification given. Complete silence followed. Everyone looked at Socrates, full of expectation. He went very calmly, almost completely relaxed, to the place where he was to speak, and began. He began the so-called defense speech. That he did not use the more or less prescribed, or at least usual, mode of address – that is something people would have found acceptable; and many hadn't even noticed. He said simply: "Men of Athens" – as if it were some kind of gathering of citizens, as if he were not before the court! But then came his irony – you know what I mean. He said that what the plaintiffs had presented was quite fascinating. He, at least, had been deeply impressed, and it wouldn't have been any different for the rest of them. But of course, he said, there was not an iota of truth in any of it. *Phaedo covers his face with his hands and shakes his head.*

ECHECRATES: And then, what happened then?

PHAEDO: Naturally there was a tremendous uproar. *With a broad gesture across the square*: In a moment this man had brought the whole kettle to the boil.

ECHECRATES: The courtroom full of children, and the doctor is the defendant.

PHAEDO: How do you mean?

ECHECRATES: I heard him say that himself – I don't know how many years ago. Was it fifteen or twenty years? He said it to Callicles. You will hardly have known him. At that time he was a very powerful man.[3]

PHAEDO *laughing*: Twenty years ago! I was just starting school.

ECHECRATES: "Do you want to know, dear Callicles," Socrates said – I remember it fairly accurately – "do you want to know why I think in such a case I would find my death?" Strangely they were talking about a court case in which Socrates could become involved. In fact, nothing of the kind was anywhere in evidence. It was a completely hypothetical supposition. So it seemed.

PHAEDO: But why a courtroom full of children?

ECHECRATES: "Imagine a doctor" – he said – a doctor taken to court by a confectioner of sweets. And the courtroom consists of children. And the doctor tries to defend himself: cutting and burning and bitter medicine – all of that is part of the healing process – how much noise do you think these judges would make? And now it turned out to be true.

PHAEDO: "Not so much noise, Athenians" – yes, that's what he said several times. But, when it's all said and done, he provoked the noise himself. The whole thing was one single provocation. You should have heard it. I would make you despair. None of us has understood why, for example, he insisted on speaking about this unfortunate Chairephon story.

ECHECRATES: Chairephon?

PHAEDO: One of his earliest followers. He is already dead. The only name we had for him was "the bat." He had become excessively gaunt through sheer fanaticism. Chairephon saw Socrates as a divine being. One day he actually came back from Delphi with the statement: Apollo himself called Socrates the wisest of all men. Fortunately, that had all been long since forgotten. But Socrates dug it up again, in great detail, with persistence, unswervingly. And naturally the noise became ever more threatening. *Grimly quoting*: "Please, no noise, Athenians!" It was amazing that they still listened to him at all.

In the meantime, the image of Socrates becomes visible. He is standing to one side behind Phaedo, far enough away from him that the camera can catch them both together or separately from one another. Echecrates cannot see Socrates, nor does he hear his voice directly but only through Phaedo's report.

Insofar as Echecrates appears at all while Socrates speaks, he is sitting, deep in his thoughts, listening to Phaedo. During the first words of Socrates the camera remains focused solely on Phaedo who is listening like someone recalling his memories, confirming, acknowledging the memory [yes, that's exactly how it was!], and becoming excited again. From time to time it is Phaedo's or Echecrates's turn to speak. As they do, Socrates's voice gradually becomes inaudible.

SOCRATES: Don't make such a fuss, men of Athens, my co-citizens! I was not the one who said it. It comes from the god in Delphi. Surely he deserves to be believed. His oracle said: no one is wiser than Socrates! What a mysterious statement, I said to myself. What can the god possibly mean? Since there is no trace of wisdom in me! And so I investigated – and thereby I made myself hated by all. I went off and asked wise people – or rather those who are taken to be wise, either by others or by themselves: politicians, writers, experts in the practical sphere. While doing this I found out the strangest thing. It turned out that in each case I was the tiniest bit wiser than they. Of course, they knew many things that I don't know. But wisdom? What is truly worth knowing – of that they know as little as I do. The only difference was that they thought they knew, whereas I was aware of not knowing. And that it was exactly this tiny bit that put me ahead of them.

God alone possesses true wisdom. Human wisdom, on the other hand, means nothing at all. That is what the oracle's statement means. It is not at all referring to Socrates. What is meant is this: anyone who, like Socrates, knows that his wisdom is worth nothing, is the wisest amongst you men.

But please don't forget why I am speaking of this. I want to make it comprehensible for you where this rage and animosity is coming from. The real reason for it has not been named. They can't bring themselves to do it. They will never admit how Socrates exposed them in their own eyes and unmasked them as people who think they are wise and yet are not. And now they are taking their revenge on me. They have been talking to you for a long time now [I know it quite well], spreading their calumnies. Unfortunately not without success. So that I don't have much hope of disabusing you of these impressive lies. The accusations were so brilliantly formulated and set out that I almost believed them myself! Not a word of truth in them – but wonderfully done! But the truth, precisely the truth is the reason they hate me. Their hatred is almost proof that I am speaking the truth.

ECHECRATES *standing up slowly and looking at Phaedo*: That is unbelievable!

PHAEDO: But that was just the beginning. A fairly harmless beginning. He then went through the list of accusations, point by point. Meletos had read it out.
Echecrates shrugs his shoulders questioningly, intimating that he doesn't know Meletos.
A completely insignificant man. A flashy literary type. You'd almost feel sorry for him. Socrates summoned him like a schoolboy. "Come here and answer my questions." He was so taken aback that he actually came. He came with his hooked nose and boy's beard.

It was a cruel game. "Are you not confusing me with someone else? With Anaxagoras, for example?" The more pitifully Meletos answered the more exaggerated the praise that Socrates showered on him. "Wonderfully said, by Hera!" – "Still so young and yet much wiser than myself at my age!"

Echecrates shakes his head in disbelief.

And as Meletos tries to defend himself – with an unbelievably silly argument – Socrates made the pretence of being terrified: "Oh, that was a really heavy blow!"

People began to laugh at Meletos. And so it went on. Finally he simply dismissed him. "No, Meletos is truly not the one" – this again said to his judges – "no, Meletos is not the one who will bring me down, if I am to be brought down. What will bring me down is the hatred of the many!" And the laughter stopped suddenly.

"If I am to be brought down" – this was repeated again and again. He was not in the slightest bent on saving himself. We were beginning to sense that the situation was now extremely serious.

Socrates begins to speak again. At first he is invisible.

SOCRATES: Let us suppose you would say to me: Good, Socrates, this time we won't listen to your accusers. You are free – under one condition. The condition is that you change your life. This so-called search for truth and wisdom – you have to give it up. And if we catch you at it again, you will die. – My answer to this would be as follows: Due respect to your friendliness, dear co-citizens, but obey? I will obey the deity and not you! As long as I draw breath I will not cease my

search for truth. Nor will I cease to appeal to your con-
science. Whomever I happen to encounter I shall ad-
monish and ask: Are you not ashamed, you, an
Athenian, a citizen of this famous city – famed for its
culture and power – are you not ashamed to be out
after nothing but money and fame and to have no concern with truth, insight, and goodness? And if someone answers me that he does care about all of these
things – then I will not let him go, oh no! I will test him
very carefully and take him into my prayers. That is
the service I owe to the divinity.

But you and your city have never been granted a
greater good than this service and this continual insistence by me that virtue does not come from wealth,
but, on the contrary, that wealth comes from virtue –
wealth and everything else that is of use to yourselves
and the whole city.

But if I corrupt the youth with such talk, then let such
damage happen. In any case, I speak of nothing else
but this, and if anyone says I do – he doesn't know
what he is talking about.

And so, citizens of Athens, judge that my accusers are
right or that I am right, acquit me or condemn me:
whatever you say, I will do nothing else – even if I had
to die several deaths!

I am not defending myself for my own sake. Don't
think that. Far from it. And I shall not attempt to
arouse your sympathy in the usual way. People in
these circumstances produce their small children, and
so on, as if they would be immortal if only this death
sentence were to be waived. Whether or not I am
afraid of dying– that is, of course, an entirely different
question. I, too, am not made of rock or oak. I, too,

have sons, three sons, two of them still children. But I will not beg you to acquit me. I leave it to you and to the divinity to judge me as is right and good – good not only for me but also for yourselves.

PHAEDO *staring in front of himself with a kind of bitter satisfaction*:
Immediately after this last sentence began the first vote of the five hundred.

ECHECRATES: The vote as to guilty or not guilty.

PHAEDO: Yes. – Of course, in our minds there was no further doubt what the result would be. But Socrates – do you know how he reacted to the vote? He was surprised above all by one thing, he said: that the vote against him was so tight! – But the worst was yet to come. The worst thing was the punishment he sought for himself.

ECHECRATES: The accused makes a suggestion for his own punishment?

PHAEDO: Yes, this is in accordance with the trial procedure. In Athens that is the case. – But do you know what Socrates said? Oh no, he did not intend to take on himself something he knew would be for him a disaster. Life in prison, for instance, he would not envisage for himself ["What would I want with the life of a slave!"] A fine? It would come to the same thing. He has no money and would have to go to prison again. Banishment? So that sooner or later he would end up in the same situation – but in a foreign place? No! Above all, he has done no injustice to anyone and so he is not about to do any injustice to himself.
If he were required to say honestly what he himself thinks he has deserved, then he would ask to take part

in the festive meal for the guests of honor of the city of Athens! – It was pure mischief. We looked at one another horrified, completely stunned. And then we were simply gripped with anger at this wonderful, dreadful man.

ECHECRATES: But what could you do? Were you close to him?

PHAEDO: Yes! Some of us sprang up and went to him, offering him sums of money and guarantees, and finally, with some effort, brought him to the point of saying that he was at least prepared to pay a reasonable fine. But, of course, it was now already too late. You know, don't you, how the second vote went?

ECHECRATES *bewildered and nodding pensively*: And how did Socrates take it?

PHAEDO: Socrates made his final speech unbowed. Anyone who heard it could not possibly forget it. It is hard to believe, but it is the exact truth: he was in perfect agreement! "I don't doubt that is the best for me if I die right away!"

SOCRATES: No, I am not sorry I defended myself in this way. To escape death now, I think, would not have been particularly difficult. But to escape badness – that is difficult! It runs more quickly than death. Now the slower one has caught up with me, me, the slow old man. But my accusers, these agile young men, have been overtaken by the quicker one: badness. And as well, co-citizens, it is only a very short span of time that I would have had to live – without your judgment. And for the sake of this short span of time you will now achieve sad fame – with those, namely, who want to denigrate our city. You have killed Socrates, they will say, this wise man! For naturally they will call me a wise man, even though I am not. You only had to wait a little while and your wish would have been fulfilled of itself. – That is what I have to say to those who have condemned me.

But to the rest of you judges [I now really do call you my judges] I have something to say while I am still free: Face death full of hope, you too! There is one thing you have to know and hold on to as indestructible truth: for one who wants the good there is no ill – neither in life nor in death. The gods will not lose sight of his cause.

And I have another thing to ask of you: if, when my sons grow up it becomes apparent that they think more about earning money than about doing good, or that they think they have knowledge and don't have it; or that they are something they are not – then take retribution: do to them the same as has happened to you at my hands.

But now it is time for us to go – I to my death, and you to life. *He turns away, but then turns back again.* Of course, who is going to a better thing is hidden from everyone – except God.

Echecrates looks at Phaedo, deeply upset. He is incapable of speaking. Phaedo sits there motionless, his elbows resting on his knees. He is staring at the ground. With a deep sigh he continues with his report.

PHAEDO: Socrates was right. As he said: death traveled very slowly. Dying was to take a good while yet. And so we began to hope again. Besides, the Athenians were afterwards a little ashamed of the death sentence.

Amongst the five hundred judges there was an increasing number who would have found it right if, for whatever reason, it had not ended in an execution.

ECHECRATES: We were saying: if only the vote could have been put off for one single day it would have turned out otherwise. Is that true?
Phaedo nods pensively.
But then, sorry –I don't understand …

PHAEDO *quickly and hotly*: The hindrance was Socrates himself, no one else! The only person in whom we could place any semblance of hope was Crito!

ECHECRATES: Crito? Who was Crito?

PHAEDO: Surely you know him. You must have met him.

ECHECRATES: That could be. But then it is years ago. And, of course, I was never in Athens for any length of time.

PHAEDO: Crito, well, anyone who sees him would not readily expect he could have anything to do with Socrates. A quite unphilosophical type! But they have been friends since childhood. The strangest friendship one could think of. I think Crito saw Socrates as a flamboyant child for whom he felt responsible – like an old experienced serving maid. And Socrates …

ECHECRATES *interrupting*: And Socrates accepted it?

PHAEDO *smiling, somewhat doubtful*: Well … Anyway, he let Crito say things to him that none of the rest of us would have dared to say. – Above all, this Crito is a marvelous organizer. You can depend on his always knowing exactly the people one needs at the time.

Anyway, to put it briefly, one day "everything was ready." Crito had hardly said a word about it.

ECHECRATES: Everything ready – for his flight? For his escape from prison?

PHAEDO: Yes! And by now it was certainly high time. So Crito went to Socrates in the prison. He told us all about it afterwards. Or rather, we gradually got it out of him.

In the meantime the inside of the prison has become visible; a long, bleak corridor, on either side doors to the cells. It is twilight. Crito and the warden come slowly downstage, in silence. Crito stops, looking around to orient himself. He points questioningly in a particular direction. The warden shakes his head obsequiously and points in the opposite direction.

Shortly before they reach Socrates's cell they stop again; Crito gives the warden money, which he quickly pockets; he expresses his thanks with a certain servility. Then he opens the cell and lets Crito enter. That all happens cautiously and without a sound.

In the cell there is a table and three or four prison beds, all empty except one. By each bed there is a stool. On the table a few books and a small stack of papers, obviously manuscripts. High up on the longer wall a row of windows. It is somewhat darker than in the corridor.

Socrates is lying under a blanket. He is asleep. His jacket is on the stool and under it his shoes. Later it can be seen that he is dressed in trousers and a collarless shirt fastened at the neck with an old-fashioned collar stud.

The warden goes out and closes the door. With cautious steps, Crito immediately goes back to the door to ascertain that it is not locked. Then he looks around the cell and,

nodding pensively, contemplates the sleeping Socrates. Finally he sits down on an empty stool and waits.
After a while Socrates suddenly wakes up. He sits up and recognizes Crito.

SOCRATES: Oh, it's you Crito? Have you been here long?
Crito nods, in control and relaxed.
Why didn't you wake me up immediately? You just sat down quietly!

CRITO: I was watching you sleeping so peacefully. I didn't want to shorten at least this lovely time for you.

SOCRATES: But why have you come so early?
He looks up at the windows. Isn't it still very early?

CRITO: Yes, it is nearly twilight.

SOCRATES: I am surprised that they have let you in already.

CRITO *laughs silently, makes a dismissive gesture and then says with undisguised irony*: Perhaps I gave the man something?

SOCRATES: All right. But why this early hour?

CRITO: I have some bad news. Bad for us, anyway?
Socrates sits upright and puts his feet on the floor.

SOCRATES: Has the ship returned?

CRITO: Not yet. But it will probably come today. And so, tomorrow …
He looks over at Socrates, observing him and waiting. Socrates stands up, puts on his shoes and jacket. He doesn't let Crito see his face.

SOCRATES: So I say: good luck! – If that's what the gods want, then so be it.
After some hesitation he casts a side-long glance at Crito.
But … I don't think the ship will come today.

CRITO: And how would you know that?

SOCRATES: I had a dream earlier. Perhaps it was better that you didn't wake me.
Crito is skeptical. In his voice a trace of impatience.

CRITO: And what did you dream?

SOCRATES: A woman called out something to me – she was beautiful, charming, dressed in white. She said something like: Another three days, and then you will …
At the last words he looks past Crito; his eyes narrow, he becomes silent, pensive, and deeply serious. Crito answers with casual politeness; he does not want to engage with this subject.

CRITO: Strange! An unusual dream.

SOCRATES: Above all, I think it is completely clear. Not tomorrow, but the day after …
Crito springs up and goes to Socrates; he speaks, although whispering, with strong emphasis.

CRITO: No! You strange man, Socrates! It is still not too late. You only have to come with me.
With quick strides he goes to the door with the face of a man bringing unexpected good news. He opens the door slightly, closes it again, and looks triumphantly at Socrates.

Socrates has watched him, full of astonishment and then goes in silence to his bed, where he carefully and without hurry folds the blanket. Finally he sits down and looks at

Crito's ironically questioning face. Crito approaches him, draws up a stool and begins again to speak with great insistence, although still almost whispering.

CRITO: Do you not understand that it is a disaster for me if you die? – And besides, people will find it very strange that we didn't have the gumption to get you out of here. That you yourself didn't want – people won't believe us if we tell them that!

SOCRATES: "People!" Crito, why are we worried about "people?"

CRITO: But surely you can see now how much we have to worry about them. They can do bad things to you.

SOCRATES: No, they can't. The worst thing that anyone can …
Crito jumps up and interrupts him, full of impatience. He doesn't want any theoretical speeches.

CRITO: But we've got everything prepared! In Thessaly I have friends with whom you will be completely safe. But there are also other places you can go. You will be welcome everywhere. *He notices that Socrates remains unimpressed, and starts again:* Besides, I think it's wrong not to save oneself when it's possible. You are doing exactly what your enemies want. And your sons? You are going away and leaving them in the lurch. – This trial – how has it been conducted? And then, to end with, this absurdity: your friends don't manage to set you free.
Crito turns away angrily. Socrates stands up slowly. Apparently slightly ruffled, he walks around in the cell while

Crito watches him tensely. Finally Socrates begins to answer. His face is turned away, he is hesitant but quite definite.

SOCRATES: Your concern for me, Crito, is fine and worthy of my gratitude – on the assumption that it is in accord with what is right. If it is not – then it is, despite everything, very questionable. I would almost say: the more active it is, the worse it is! Let us discuss whether or not I should act according to your advice.
Crito sits down at the table with a gesture of resignation, chin resting in his hand. He is silently looking past Socrates. Socrates sits down with him and continues speaking to him in a friendly tone.
So, how does it stand with the convictions we have so often spoken of? Were they only correct as long as this death sentence wasn't there? Whereas it has now become clear that it only amounted to a kind of conversation? A game? Chat? And we have grown old and haven't realized that?

CRITO: Of course that is not the case.

SOCRATES: So it is still true: "The fundamental good does not consist in our simply remaining alive but in living a good life"?

CRITO: Yes, of course that still stands. It still applies!

SOCRATES: And what about wrongdoing? Is it in no way permissible? Or does it depend on "circumstances?" Does our old saying still apply: "Wrongdoing is never permissible"?

CRITO *becoming ever more convinced that he is fighting a losing battle*: The saying is still valid.

SOCRATES: And also, if wrong is done to us we are still not entitled to do wrong ourselves?

CRITO *now almost entirely disengaging and giving purely routine answers*: No, we are not.

SOCRATES: Think carefully, Crito. If that is not really your opinion then don't agree with me! I know very well that very few people are of this opinion – and will be!

CRITO: It really is my opinion.

SOCRATES: Then let's continue. Must we honor contracts?

CRITO: Yes, we must.

SOCRATES: And if I go with you now – are we not then breaking a contract?

CRITO *evincing new interest. He thinks he sees the possibility of perhaps convincing Socrates after all*: I don't understand your question. How do you mean?

SOCRATES: Let us suppose we were really to run off from here –
Crito wants to protest against this expression, but Socrates continues in an energetically appeasing tone.
Running off, or whatever else you like to call it. And now the laws get in our way – the law of our city of Athens, and Athens itself. Imagine that they would ask us some questions: "Tell us, Socrates, what you have in mind? Do you think a state can have stability if someone or other, an individual, can negate a court judgment?" What are we then to say? Is our answer to be: But this state has done us an injustice?

CRITO: That's exactly what we will say, naturally.

SOCRATES: But the laws would reply: "Obviously you have been satisfied with us and the state. You have never left the city of Athens except for campaigns. Unlike other people, you have never made a journey to any other place. Above all: during the court proceedings you were still free to apply for banishment! And so with permission from the state you could have done legally what you now want to do illegally. But then you were playing the big man as if dying meant nothing to you. And now you are putting all that out of your mind and you want to creep away secretly like a slave in some kind of ludicrous disguise. And our agreement, according to which you promised to live here as a citizen – that is suddenly no longer valid?

Crito has stood up and walks, resigned and pensive, a few steps towards the door. He turns his back on Socrates. After a lengthy silence Socrates goes to him.

SOCRATES: My dear friend! I think I am constantly hearing such questions. And everything else is drowned out by them. – Besides, didn't you yourself, Crito, give your guarantee that I will remain here?[4]
Crito turns away again in silent sadness and sits on a stool as far away from Socrates as possible. Socrates follows him with his gaze and contemplates him for a long time. Finally Crito stands up, embraces Socrates, and leaves the cell.
As we see him wandering pensively and hesitantly down the long corridor and finally turning to leave through the exit, Phaedo, still invisible, continues his report. The prison corridor remains in view, now in broad daylight; from time to time we see a warden in the distance.

PHAEDO: Crito had been too sure. And when his main argument – "the door is open!" made no impression he simply gave up. In the end, so he said, Socrates asked him whether he had any further arguments for him …

ECHECRATES *animated*: I can just imagine. I can see Socrates as if he were here in front of me, saying: "Now my dear man, do you have anything else to propose?" He looks you straight in the face. With kind irony, so to speak. And you'd be standing there like a schoolboy.

PHAEDO: Now Crito is not so easily intimidated. He was simply disappointed beyond measure. And so he said: No, I've said everything.

ECHECRATES: So that was the end of that?

PHAEDO: Yes. We were all dumbfounded. This man! We still admired him; but we didn't understand him. None of us considered death unavoidable – or having any sense. We did find this obstinacy somehow marvelous; but it was still obstinacy after all. Socrates himself knew very well what we thought of him. He said it to us quite bluntly when we came to take leave of him.
Gradually his friends arrive in the corridor of the prison; some of them are wearing summer raincoats from which they are shaking off the drops of rain; they throw them afterwards on one of the empty beds. Some have pulled up their coat collars. Phaedo and Apollodorus come first, accompanied by the warden who opens the cell door for them. He waits standing outside the door. After a while Simmias and Cebes come from the prison gate into the corridor. A second warden shows them the direction; meanwhile the conversation between Phaedo and Echecrates continues.

ECHECRATES: That was on the last day?

PHAEDO: Yes. Besides, Socrates's dream had turned out to be right: it was the third day since the fruitless conversation with Crito. The ship did not, in fact, come back as early as had been expected.

ECHECRATES: What did you speak about? What did Socrates say? And who was there besides you? Surely Crito too?

PHAEDO: Crito was the last to arrive. Apollodorus and I were the first.

ECHECRATES: Apollodorus! I know the name, of course. Isn't he the "crazy one?"

PHAEDO: Yes, that's what some people call him.[5] But I don't. He is somewhat effusive, and he is exaggerated in his expression of feeling. And naturally that came to the fore at this moment; it was sometimes hard to take. However, I do like him. There is nothing false in him.

ECHECRATES: Well, I've got nothing against him.

PHAEDO: Fortunately both the Thebans came, Simmias and Cebes. Socrates always enjoyed their unbelievable appetite for debate. Even on a day like this they were not able to control it. The argument lasted almost into the evening.

ECHECRATES: And what was it about? Tell me.

PHAEDO: At first the conversation was slow to get going. It was an unpleasant day. The rain was coming down in torrents. We were wet through.
Socrates's cell can now be seen. He is sitting on his bed, his knees drawn up. Phaedo is already there; he is sitting

on a stool beside Socrates. Apollodorus is standing around helplessly. Simmias and Cebes greet Socrates silently either by a handshake or an embrace. A bed is pulled up; Simmias sits down on it, while Cebes goes to the table with the manuscripts. Meantime, Phaedo continues with his report.

PHAEDO: Above all, we were ourselves, as you can imagine, in a strange frame of mind. There was Socrates sitting in front of us, quite calm, almost cheerful. And yet we knew that that evening he would be dead. But strangely – I can, of course, only speak for myself – I think none of us was really sad. Although every now and then we were in tears. Certainly Apollodorus was completely beside himself; he could not manage, during the whole time, to speak a word. – So at first we were standing around not knowing quite what to do. What should we talk about? Socrates didn't make it any easier for us with his somewhat amused, questioning eyes. And when finally Cebes, in his slightly Theban way of speaking,[6] broke the silence, everyone breathed a sigh of relief. He himself seemed really happy that this comical figure of Evenus occurred to him, the fashionable writer-philosopher whom Socrates had already made fun of in court.[7]

Socrates looks around the group, nodding pensively but with a degree of cheerfulness. Cebes, who has been looking at the books and papers, turns around to Socrates with a couple of manuscript pages in his hand.

CEBES: You are now suddenly writing verse! Some people have been surprised to know that. Evenus recently asked me about it, saying you have always disdained to do that kind of thing.

At the mention of the name of Evenus all react with a laugh of ironic amusement. Socrates also laughs briefly but interrupts Cebes.

SOCRATES: Evenus! Calm him down; tell him I have no intention of competing with him in his poetry. He has nothing to fear from me.
There is some forced laughter; but the mood of depression cannot be lifted. Socrates himself suddenly becomes serious again.
So, give my greetings to Evenus; and tell him that if he is wise he will soon follow me – to the place to which I will go, and indeed, as far as one can see, as soon as today. Because that's what the Athenians want.

CEBES *puts the manuscript back on the table and at first speaks more or less to himself*: Evenus! He will say thank you very much! He wouldn't dream of it!

SOCRATES *slyly ironic*: And so he's not a philosopher?

CEBES: And a philosopher is, in your opinion, someone who wishes to die? What is that about? – Besides, I find that strange: death is supposed to be a good thing, but one is not allowed to take this good thing for himself. And what would be the reason for that?

SOCRATES: Yes, that is a question to which I have no proper answer – at least not my own. On the basis of what I have heard, naturally I know an answer. I won't keep it from you if you'd like to know it.

CEBES: Well, that one is not allowed to take one's own life – I've heard that said many a time. But: why not? I've never heard anything enlightening on that score.

SOCRATES: It is indeed difficult to understand that we are not allowed to do a good deed to ourselves; that, instead, we have to wait for someone else, for a benefactor.

CEBES: That's exactly what I mean.

SOCRATES: The answer of which I am speaking has its origin in the mysteries; and it seems to me worthy of careful consideration. The answer is as follows: we human beings are one of the herds of the gods, the gods are our custodians. And for this reason we are not allowed, of ourselves, to make off. We have to wait until the gods decree it – like now, as in my case. – Perhaps that doesn't seem so unreasonable?

CEBES: No. But then it really is unreasonable that the wise should be aiming at death. Why would they wish to leave the herd of the gods?

SOCRATES *who has listened to this argument with an expression of admiration and respect and obvious pleasure*: This fellow Cebes! He always digs up counter arguments! And it is not easy to convince him!

SIMMIAS: But I think he is right this time. What kind of reason can there be for a wise man to want to leave his divine custodians? They are surely much better than he is himself. *He looks at Socrates. It is friendly challenge.* We are speaking about you, Socrates! It is you we mean! That you find it so easy to leave us!

SOCRATES *looks questioningly and in bewilderment from Simmias to Cebes, and then, after a deep sigh*: All right! I will try to defend myself – against you? Against my friends! Good. Hopefully I'll have more success with you than with the judges.

He looks silently into space for a while and then begins again, with obvious caution and formulating precisely.
Certainly it would not have been right to go confidently to my death if I were not absolutely sure that there were gods also on the other side. And, in general … that beyond … there is something for the dead; that something is prepared for them there. But I am convinced of that: the greatest of good things await us on the other side of death. And it is for that reason that those who truly philosophize are fundamentally out after nothing but their death.
Simmias can't suppress a laugh, for which he immediately apologizes.

SIMMIAS: God knows, I don't feel like laughing. But I have to think of what people would say if they heard something like that. They would probably say: Yes, we've known for a long time that philosophers deserve death!

SOCRATES *serious, but not criticizing*: "People" know nothing at all – neither that the philosophizers yearn for death, nor that they deserve it, nor what kind of death! But let's forget about the people.
What does "death" mean? And what does the philosophizer wish for? "Death"? And do we mean by that the separation of body and soul?

SIMMIAS: Naturally – what else?

SOCRATES: And the philosophizer? Is he particularly concerned with the so-called nice things of life? Eating and drinking, sensual pleasure, clothes, jewelry – or anything else of this kind?
He looks Simmias in the eye. Simmias shakes his head.

But people, the many, are they not of the opinion that one is not really "alive" if one sets no store by those things? That one is in fact already as good as dead?

SIMMIAS: Agreed. That's what I said!

SOCRATES *who does not want to return to this theme*: Let's move on. Beauty, justice, greatness, the essence of things – did you ever see any of these things with your own eyes?

SIMMIAS: No.

SOCRATES: Or did you ever grasp any of them with one of the other senses in your body?

SIMMIAS: Even less.

SOCRATES: To arrive at such knowledge must one not, on the contrary, remove oneself as far as possible from all to do with the senses and the corporeal?

SIMMIAS: Yes.

SOCRATES: But this removal and turning away from the body, this "separation" – is that not already almost death? And thus pure knowing amounts to being carried away by the goddess of death? But then why, since we want to know the truly real – why resist when death really comes to us?
Ah, there is Crito! Greetings!
Crito enters quickly. He greets Socrates with a handshake and puts a hand on his shoulder.
That's good. So, no ill feelings?

CRITO *with a slightly defensive gesture*: What ill feelings? ...
He soon goes back to the door. From time to time he turns around to speak with the warden.

SOCRATES *turning back to Simmias*: This is what I could, for example, produce in my defense. Will you accept it, Simmias and Cebes? Or what do you think?

CEBES: All you have just said, Socrates, seems correct – but for one thing. It must still be proved, I think, that the soul, at the moment it leaves the body, does not simply pass away – like a breath of air or like smoke. If it did still have existence – an existence in its own right – then we could hope for many glorious things. But what are the arguments here?

SOCRATES: You are quite right, Cebes. – But what are we to do now? Continue our discussion or just leave it here?
Socrates, Simmias and Cebes look around to the others.

CEBES: No! I, for one, would like to know your views on this.

SOCRATES: Fine. If you wish ... But what has Crito been wanting to say all the time?
Crito has taken a step towards Socrates with the obvious intention of telling him something. But he shrinks from interrupting the conversation. He now leans against the doorpost again, his hands behind his back. In response to Socrates's question he points with his head in the direction of the corridor and then answers with a somewhat forced casualness.

CRITO: The warden out there is throwing his weight around. He keeps on saying to me you should talk as little as possible. It has something to do with the effects of this ... drink. Otherwise you would have to drink it twice, or even three times.

SOCRATES: Tell him to mind his own business. Let him give me the cup twice, even three times if necessary.

CRITO: I almost knew that already. But he left me no peace.

SOCRATES *with a gesture signaling closure he turns back to Simmias and Cebes*: All right. What about the souls of the dead? Where are they then?
He pauses, and starts anew. What follows now sounds like mere quotation; it becomes clear that Socrates himself does not embrace the idea.
It used to be said that souls not only go over there, but that they also come from there – from the realm of the dead back to life. If that were the case our souls would have to have an existence there. Of course, if it is not the case …

CEBES *who has several times wanted to say something, now interrupts Socrates*: But, what you are always saying yourself – namely, that learning is nothing other than remembering: and that means that already before this life we must have experienced something – precisely that which we are now remembering!

SIMMIAS: But can that be proved?

CEBES: There is the following argument and not a bad one, I think: you only have to ask people about things – things they don't already know, of course, as in mathematics. You don't instruct them, you just ask questions, and voilà! – they give the correct answer of themselves. And so they already knew it in some way or other. It's just that they had forgotten it.

SOCRATES *to Simmias*: You obviously have your doubts: learning is nothing but remembering ... ?

SIMMIAS *laughing*: No, I don't have any doubts really. Only ... I can't quite remember!

SOCRATES *serious again after a short laugh*: But we are agreed on one thing: you don't speak of remembering except when you have already had some kind of knowledge beforehand?

SIMMIAS: Of course not. That is clear.

SOCRATES: Good. We see two pieces of wood or two stones. And we say: they are "equally" big; or: they have the "same" color. Do we not know already what "equal" means before we see anything with our eyes?

SIMMIAS: Yes, that seems to be the case.

SOCRATES: So, before we began to see and to hear, that is, before we were born, we already knew what equality is but also what beauty, goodness, and justice are – and so forth!
Simmias nods.
Then the soul must also have had an existence – before birth! Non-corporeal, spiritual being.

SIMMIAS: I don't know what I can say against that.

SOCRATES: And what does Cebes say?

CEBES: I say: one half is clear. But only a half. Before birth our soul has already existed. But: how does it stand afterwards, after death? At least here nothing has as yet been proven.
Simmias nods in agreement.

SOCRATES *smiling*: So you are a little afraid that the wind could blow your soul away as soon as it leaves its house.

CEBES *first laughing but then serious*: State your argument as if we were really afraid. – But perhaps I should not say "as if." Perhaps there is a child in us that is afraid. And we have to try to take away its fear.

SOCRATES: All right! So the question is: to what things can it happen that they break up and evaporate?
He looks at Simmias and Cebes; but they say nothing.
Can anything that is simple be broken up – or only something that is composite?

CEBES: Obviously only what is composite, not the simple.

SOCRATES: Next. Can we say: that which remains always the same is probably also simple? But anything that changes is composite?

CEBES *hesitantly*: At least that's the way it seems.

SOCRATES: Another step: is the soul not cognate mainly with what remains the same, with the simple, intransitory, incorporeal, immortal, divine – but the body mainly with what is changeable, transitory and mortal? Or can there be any objection to this?

CEBES *hesitant again*: No, it would seem.

Socrates stands up, puts his shoes on and, deep in thought, paces up and down for a bit. Then he remains standing at the table and, obviously thinking of something else, is putting his papers in order. Simmias and Cebes have also stood up. They go into the opposite corner of the cell and put their heads together, whispering. Socrates becomes aware of them and looks back at them over his shoulder.

SOCRATES: Have you found something else? Naturally, when you consider everything carefully there's a lot left to say.

Simmias and Cebes have become somewhat embarrassed and are silent. Socrates continues, in a good mood:

Or are you speaking about something different? If any case, if any new doubts have occurred to you tell me about them. So that I can help you – if there is anything you expect of me.

Simmias looks at Cebes and then, as if he has plucked up courage, goes to Socrates.

SIMMIAS: It is true. We do in fact have objections, each of us a different one. But … we really didn't want to talk any more about them. *He speaks hesitantly. He is unsure and is concerned to find the right word.* We don't want to … unsettle you … in this awful situation. Perhaps it will only distress you …

Socrates nods and smiles as if he has been confirmed in something. Then he turns to face Simmias full on.

SOCRATES: Heavens! Simmias! What you are saying is very bad, very bad indeed. Fancy my not being able to convince even you! If so, how can I make it clear to others, the "people," that I don't consider my situation awful! Do you think so little of me?

Swans, when they feel that death is near – they sing! For joy! That they are now to come to the god whose servants they are. Men in their fear of death say about the swans that their song is a lamentation – as if any bird would sing when it is hungry or freezing or when anything else is wrong with him. No, swans sing

because Apollo makes them sense the joy of Hades.
But I, too, am in the service of this same god. And he
has given, also to me, the gift of being a seer. I am no
less happy than the swans are to leave this life.
So, speak and ask what you think is necessary and for as
long as you like – or: as long as the Athenians permit!
*In saying these last words with great seriousness, Socrates
has placed his hands on the table with the palms facing up-
wards. Now he gives Simmias a friendly smile. As they both
continue to be silent, Socrates turns to them again.*
So, what kind of objections do you have?

SIMMIAS *at first faltering and clearly embarrassed*: Could
one not, I ask myself, say something similar about the
soul and the body to what we say about the melody
and the lyre? Music, harmony, melody – all of that is
incorporeal, glorious, divine; whereas the lyre and the
strings are physical things, composite, earthly, mortal.
You have sometimes said it yourself: our body is like
a lyre and the soul is like melody and harmony. But
now: if someone breaks the lyre and the strings – does
not the music then vanish? The soul, too –no matter
how "divine" it is?
*Socrates looks into space. Then he nods respectfully to Sim-
mias.*

SOCRATES: That sounds good. How can one – does any
of you know the answer?
*He looks at them all, one after the other. All are silent,
clearly not knowing what to say.*
We have to save time. And perhaps Cebes should also
tell us his objection.

CEBES: Yes, I have a few doubts about whether we've
made any Evenus progress so far. The soul existing

before this life – I have no problem with that. I have also not the slightest doubt that, in comparison with the body, it is the more powerful element and "of itself" the lasting element. But, just like Simmias, I must use an image to express it. Man is clearly something greater and nobler than the garment he wears. And one can also say that the man lives longer than the garment; in the course of his life he wears out many garments. But his last garment, although inferior to him by far, does it not, however, outlive him? I think it does. And so the soul may well be the nobler element; it may wander through many bodies and wear them out like clothes. But how do we know that it, too, at the very end, does not similarly pass away?

Socrates nods several times, pensively. Then he turns to the papers lying on the table, paging through them. Finally, he goes slowly back to his bed and sits down. He puts an arm around Phaedo's shoulder and runs a hand through his long hair.

Meanwhile Echecrates and Phaedo are heard but remain invisible.

ECHECRATES *at first whispering but then continuing in normal conversational tone:* We all see it like that! –What does Socrates say now? Does everything start all over again? But is there any point? I find they are all correct.

PHAEDO: That's exactly what I thought, too. I was more or less despairing. Until then everything seemed so perfectly clear! – But also the others – we spoke about it afterwards – there was not one of us who was not convinced that arguments achieved nothing, not regarding this subject.

ECHECRATES: And Socrates?

PHAEDO: Socrates was wonderful. I have seldom found him so inspiring. Of course, he saw through us straightaway. He knew that we were about to capitulate. But he hauled us back like a crowd of deserting soldiers. And it is hard to believe: our courage was renewed.

ECHECRATES: And how did he manage that?

PHAEDO *whispering again*: Listen!

SOCRATES: And so tomorrow you will have your beautiful hair shorn?

PHAEDO *moved and sad*: Yes, Socrates, very likely.

SOCRATES: No, you won't do that if you listen to me.

PHAEDO: Why not?

SOCRATES *with feigned seriousness*: Because it has to be today. And I will have my hair shorn today – if the logos dies here, our debate, our argumentation! If we don't enliven it again – I would, in your place– like the ancient Argives – even swear an oath not to let my hair grow again before I had conquered them, both Simmias and Cebes.
Phaedo, who at first does not know what to do, is relieved and plays along with Socrates's joke.

PHAEDO: Me – one against two? Even Heracles couldn't do that.

SOCRATES: So now you have to call on my help. As long as the sun is up.

PHAEDO: Fine. I call on you!

SOCRATES *still turned to Phaedo but obviously including the others who are still listening intently*: This is the first thing: we have to take care that something particular doesn't happen to us, something very dangerous.

PHAEDO *unsure, since he doesn't know whether the game is continuing*: What? I mean, what sort of danger is there?

SOCRATES: We must be careful not to become despisers of the word.
Phaedo's expression is questioning, uncomprehending.
There are those who despise humankind, who are enemies of humankind. Both are rooted in the one thing. The contempt comes about in this way: first there is unbounded trust; anyone we find pleasing is immediately "a marvelous person." Until, a couple of times we are deeply disappointed – and suddenly there is no one in the world worth anything. – Did you never see this happen?
Phaedo nods vaguely. He is unsure.
But anyone with experience of people knows that only very few are completely bad and also that only very few are completely good.

PHAEDO in *naïve disbelief*: Really?

SOCRATES: It is the same everywhere. No matter whether it is to do with color or greatness or speed: the extreme is rare and the mean is in the majority. – But you are side-tracking me. I wanted to speak about those who hate the word. At first people accept everything they hear – without question, as long as it is well said. But then, of course, they notice that some things are not quite right. And suddenly it has happened: one is completely convinced [and sees oneself as extraordinarily wise] that there is nothing one can rely on, absolutely nothing, either in the concrete world or in words. – Have you never met such people?

PHAEDO: Oh yes! I know them well, very well.

SOCRATES: Good. That's what we have to be careful of. We won't blindly accept everything that is said, and, even more, we will never believe that there is no substance at all in words. *From here on Socrates is speaking more and more obviously to Simmias and Cebes.*
If it is a really sound argument, as I am convinced it is, it would be bad not to share in its truth.
As for myself, if my arguments in favor of immortality are really astray, I won't be in error much longer. But that cannot dispense us from further investigation. Just oppose me when you find I am wrong and don't be misled by my obstinacy. In the end I am deceiving myself and you as well. And then I fly away and, like a bee, leave the sting in you. No, if you want to listen to me don't worry about Socrates; concern yourselves about truth!
So, Simmias and Cebes, how does it stand with you? Do you reject everything I have said so far, or do you accept some of it?

CEBES: Well, for example, the argument for the pre-existence of the soul. That has completely convinced me.

SIMMIAS: Me too! Learning is remembering, and therefore the soul has known something before this life. That is for me a completely incontestable proposition.

SOCRATES: And yet you will have to give it up – if you still maintain that the body is the lyre and the soul is the music.

SIMMIAS: I don't understand.

SOCRATES: Simmias! If there is no melody after the lyre is destroyed how can it exist before there is a lyre? *Simmias is confused.*
So you have to choose. Either learning is memory; or the soul is melody.

SIMMIAS: I choose the first one. But the other one – I thought it was a brilliant argument ...

SOCRATES *interrupting him*: ... whereas in reality it is worthless. Indeed, for several reasons. For example: can a melody have control over a lyre from which it emanates? But the soul rules over the body, controls it, forms it, disciplines it, and so on.

SIMMIAS *still shaking his head at his own confusion*: Yes, yes, of course.

SOCRATES *turned to Cebes*: But what about the other argument?

CEBES: After you dismissed Simmias with such unbelievable speed, you will not, I imagine, be embarrassed for an answer in this case. I really hadn't expected that; to me his argument seemed incontrovertible. – And now it's my turn.

SOCRATES: Shush, Cebes. We must do honest battle with one another, like the fighters in Homer. What you said certainly has weight: that it is not enough to show that the soul has been in existence for a long time; one must also prove that it will not vanish in the future. – otherwise one could not face death with confidence. That is your objection, isn't it?

CEBES: Yes, that's exactly it.

Socrates stares pensively into space for a while; then he begins hesitantly.

SOCRATES: We must try to make clear ... well, in what way – in general! – anything comes into being and in what way it vanishes ... Should I tell you my own experience in this regard?

CEBES *eagerly agreeing*: Yes, we would very much like to hear about it.

Socrates draws up his legs on the bed, clasps his knees in his hands and leans his head back against the wall.

SOCRATES: When I was young I was strongly attracted to what is these days called natural science. I really wrestled with questions such as: does life really emanate, as some say, from decay? Do we think with our blood or with the brain? Does judgment and knowing come from seeing, hearing, and smelling? And how is all of this lost again? – But in the end it became clear to me: all of that leads to nothing. And I felt I was stupid and useless.

Then one day I heard someone reading aloud – from a book by Anaxagoras, as I was told. The content was: the cause of all things is spirit, reason! I could see that immediately and I was enthused to have found a teacher who suited me perfectly. So I immediately read all the writings of this man that I could lay my hands on. But my expectations, which had been so high, were completely dashed. There was no further mention of reason, but only of air and water again! It's as if someone were to say: Socrates does everything he does on the basis of reason – but then, as soon as it came down to details, I only talked of bones, muscles, tendons and joints as the cause of my sitting here with my knees drawn up...

He stands up, walks up and down and stops in front of Crito whom he looks at pointedly and somewhat slyly.

Whereas, God knows, these bones would have been long since in Megara or ... Thessaly, if reason and insight had not persuaded me not flee but to remain. And so one must clearly be able to distinguish – between the true, real cause and the conditions under which it operates.

But in order to find out about that last and true cause – of everything that is – I would joyfully have become anyone's pupil. But this hope, however, has turned out to be vain. I was neither able to find out the truth for myself, nor was I able to find it out from anyone else ...

CEBES *incredulous and amazed*: But ... what is your opinion now, today?

SOCRATES: I don't have any opinion at all! At least, I no longer think I know the true reason for anything; and I don't know what to make of the scholarly "reasons" and "causes." It seems to me that one should proceed with extreme caution in contemplating things as they are in themselves. Otherwise one could suffer the fate of those who look at the sun – and go blind.

Ultimate reality, ultimate excellence, the primary cannot, I believe, be tracked down. But ... I do believe that I really have found the second best. Should I tell you about that? Or are you becoming impatient?

CEBES: No! I'm dying to hear it!

SOCRATES *with a sly smile*: Basically, what I am about to say is not at all new. It is, yet again, what I am constantly saying. Perhaps I am really a bit simple-minded. But I hold to the idea that, for example, beautiful things are beautiful by virtue of their sharing in and being part of the ultimately beautiful itself. That is, in my opinion, the "reason" and "cause" of their being beautiful. Apart from that I understand nothing.

But I still have a residue of hope that I can enlighten you about the immortality of the soul – assuming that you admit that there is such a thing as the ultimately beautiful, the good in itself, and so on.

CEBES: You know I admit it. But now you really have my attention.

SOCRATES: Well, we are agreed that none of these can turn into its opposite? Beautiful things can become ugly and small things big. But not the beautiful itself. It always remains itself; likewise the "small in itself" – and so on. Is that clear?

CEBES: Yes, here, too, we are in agreement. Completely!

SOCRATES: And yet there are certain things, concretely existing things, which nevertheless … *He hesitates and falters.*

CEBES *after a brief silence*: … which themselves … are like "ideas."

SOCRATES: No, of course not! This is very difficult. Take fire, for example. It is not identical with "hot in itself," with the unchangeable "ultimately hot," so to speak;

but it is so closely related to it and linked with it that fire, also, can never become cold. Is that true to say?

CEBES: Yes, that is correct. But I don't see what you are driving at.

SOCRATES: Is the soul not that through which the body is alive?

CEBES *in some amazement*: Of course!

SOCRATES: And is that not always the case? If the body is to be alive the soul has to dwell within it?

CEBES: Yes, that is always the case.

SOCRATES: Therefore, wherever the soul is it brings life with it?

CEBES: It seems to be so.

SOCRATES: And what is the opposite of life?

CEBES: Death.

SOCRATES: Now, if fire never becomes cold and does not permit of cold – can the soul, which always brings life and has life with it, ever be compatible with death?

CEBES *looking uncertainly around the room*: I can't see any objection to this. But perhaps Simmias has something to say – or someone else? If that is the case I think he should speak up.

SIMMIAS *with a despairing gesture*: I'm not altogether convinced! But I don't see any objection I can bring. These things are, after all, rather complicated …

SOCRATES: You are quite right, Simmias! Even when you are completely convinced you have to re-examine your initial presuppositions again. Then you will – perhaps – arrive at certainty, step by step; to the degree of certainty that is humanly possible.

Socrates stands up, goes to the table, picks up the papers again, and finally lays them down beside the books. Then he leans against the wall, with his hands behind his back. He is staring into the distance, and he says the following words more to himself than to his friends.

But if the soul does not die … we do well to pay good attention to it.

SIMMIAS: How do you mean?

SOCRATES *pensively*: Yes, immortality is a … frightening thing.

SIMMIAS *amazed and incredulous*: A frightening thing? Immortality?

SOCRATES: Yes! – for anyone who does not want the good. Something terrifying and a horrifying danger. It would have to be, on the contrary, very welcome to him, on dying, to be simply free of everything – not just from the body but also from the soul and all its badness. But what we are ourselves, good or bad – that's what we take with us! It is the only thing we take with us into the other world.

You know the message that has been handed down to us from time immemorial. The daimon, the same one whose care the living also enjoy, leads the dead person to the place of judgment. There the verdict is spoken – about the good, no less than about the bad. Many are, of course, between both – in the middle; they have led an average life, have also done bad things but not of such a kind that no healing is possible. They are

sent to a place of purification where they atone for
their deeds and are purified of their guilt.

CEBES: Yes, I know. That is what tradition says. But – how
is that done? How is the soul "purified"?

SOCRATES: Through torment and pain! There is no other
way of ridding oneself of wrong. Neither here nor beyond![8] – But once the time of punishment is over the
souls are brought before those they have wronged;
and only when they receive pardon from them are
they free.

But those who are fundamentally bad, whose evil is
found to be beyond all healing, plunge down into Tartarus, never to return from it.

Finally, those who have lived a life pleasing to the divinity: they are free of all captivity; they are led immediately into that pure domain where, in the temple,
not the images of the gods but the gods themselves are
to be found. It will be a true dwelling together of gods
and men.

*Socrates seems to withdraw himself from this vision only
with difficulty; he is silent for a while; then he takes a deep
breath and turns to Simmias, who has walked over to him,
and gradually resumes the normal tone of conversation.*

Yes, my dear Simmias, it is worthwhile being good
and living according to one's noblest insights. What
one can then hope for is glorious beyond all measure.
– But now, that everything happens word for word as
it is described – that is something which, understandably, we cannot say.

SIMMIAS *surprised and at the same time feeling somewhat
confirmed in his opinion*: Ah, so you yourself consider
that this is only a story?

SOCRATES: No, not "only" a story! A story, yes. Symbolic speech, an allegory, an image. But this image is completely true! In all of our investigations we will find nothing of greater truth.[9] – And that this corresponds more or less to the way it will be with our souls and their dwelling place – that is something we should surely dare to believe. A good act of daring!

In any case, a person who during his lifetime [in the stretch of time that we normally call "life"] is concerned to embellish his soul not with external things but with things proper to himself: with truth, justice, bravery – such a one has nothing to fear. He can face the journey into Hades and be ready to go when the time comes.

Of course, one has to cast a spell on oneself [so to speak] and entertain such mythical stories. That's why I, too, am so long preoccupied with them and develop them ever further.

After Socrates has now spoken more to himself again and in a kind of ecstasy, he turns finally to the concrete situation and the world around him. He goes to his bed and sits down. Well, Simmias, Cebes and you others – you will not start your journey till later, each at his own appointed time. As for myself … a tragedian would say: "Fate is calling me!" – right now, at this very moment!

These last words are spoken with mock pathos in which a superior cheerfulness of soul is mixed with a not altogether successful attempt to alleviate the sadness of his friends. – Crito is the only one who, in his realistic sobriety, keeps focused on the immediate practical situation.

CRITO: All right now, Socrates. Do you have any tasks for those of us here, for me or for the others? For instance, with regard to your sons? – Or is there anything else we could do for you?

Socrates looks at him very calmly. The tone of his answer is indulgent and unwavering.

SOCRATES: Nothing else Crito, except what I have always been speaking about. Care for yourselves in the proper way – that is how you will be doing the best for me and yourselves, and also for my loved ones – even if you don't make a promise now. But if you lose sight of what is truly good for you ... *he makes a dismissive, cancelling gesture* you could promise me as much as you like, and then ...

CRITO *interrupting him impatiently*: But Socrates! Of course we will do all of that. There is no way we wouldn't! But ... *he looks around the group in some embarrassment and then resolutely raises another question which he considers to be urgent.* What are we to do ... for example, about your ... burial?

SOCRATES *with somewhat exaggerated indifference*: Oh, do whatever you like!
After a brief silence he continues, with a sly smile: Assuming that you are able to catch me! Assuming that, in the meantime, I haven't escaped you! *He laughs to himself, shakes his head, and looks around the group.* This Crito, my friends – I'm not able to convince him. He still thinks the dead body he will soon get to see is Socrates! I have said all along that I won't be there any longer when I have drunk the cup, but will be transported to the Isles of the Blessed. But he thinks I have only said that to calm myself and you as well. You must guarantee for me, just as he did for me in court, except the other way round: not that I will remain here but that, on the contrary, I will most certainly go away! Then it will be easier for him to see my body being

buried or consumed by fire. In either case nothing awful is happening to me. *He turns again to Crito.* Cheer up, Crito! It is only my body that you will be burying, and so you can do it as you think best and according to our customs.

Meanwhile the warden has entered. At first he remains near the door and lets Socrates finish his speech. Then he goes up to him. Simmias and the others make room for him. Phaedo, still unmoved but following everything very intently, is sitting on the stool next to Socrates's bed. He looks in fright at the warden.

WARDEN: I am sure, Socrates, that you won't be angry with me, as others usually are, when I have to announce that it is now time to drink the cup of hemlock. The whole time I have been convinced: never has a better man ever entered this prison. – So, you know what my task is?

Socrates nods, looking into space.

So, farewell! And try to bear the inevitable with equanimity.

The warden turns to go and quickly leaves the cell, suddenly breaking down in tears.

SOCRATES *calling after him:* Farewell to you, too! And I will do as you say. *After a silent pause, to his friends:* What a man! We have often spoken with one another. He has always been friendly to me. And now he is in tears! *To Crito:* But now we have to deal with his announcement. Crito, see to it that they bring the cup.

CRITO *slightly impatient, pointing to the still brightly-lit windows:* The sun is still above the mountains! It is not yet time. Besides, I know that many a one has delayed it for a long time. There is no hurry.

SOCRATES *with a friendly reproach*: Crito! The others would certainly have had a reason to delay. But I have a reason not to. There's nothing to gain by it. I would only become laughable in my own eyes. – So, do as I say.

Crito goes out. Everyone is silent. After a short time he comes back. The court bailiff enters, carrying the cup of hemlock in both hands.

Phaedo has sprung up from his stool; he shrinks back as far as the wall and presses his back against it. He remains like this until the end, his horrified gaze fixed steadily and full of sympathy on Socrates.

The Court Bailiff puts the cup on the table and stands near it, aware of his duty. Socrates has at first remained seated and with a serious face looks sideways over his shoulder towards the man. Then he stands up slowly and with his hands behind his back contemplates the cup.

At this moment Apollodorus has a loud fit of crying. He throws himself full length onto the bed. Crito and Phaedo try to calm him down.

SOCRATES *turning round to them*: What are you doing, you strange people! I have always been told one should be quiet when someone is dying. So, control yourselves and keep quiet. *Turning to the Bailiff:* Now, my friend, what do I have to do? You understand these things.

COURT BAILIFF *in an official but not unfriendly tone*: After you drink it you walk around until your legs become heavy. Then you lie down.

SOCRATES: What do you think? Can one offer a libation to gods with this drink?

COURT BAILIFF: The cup contains only the necessary amount!

SOCRATES: I understand. But a prayer is permissible?
The bailiff shrugs his shoulders uncomprehendingly.
Socrates continues, now speaking more quietly to himself:
It is even required! One must ask the gods that the transition from here to the beyond is a happy one.
He looks around the room and fixes his eye on the door, the window, the bed, as well as on his friends, in wonderment.
This is what I will now ask for.
He folds his arms, clasping his elbows in his hands, closes his eyes for a moment, and takes a deep breath.
Let it happen now!
Then, now in his own world, he takes the cup and puts it to his lips in silence.
Meanwhile, with the whispering voice of Socrates himself, a sentence from his defense speech is repeated:

VOICE OF SOCRATES: "I, too, am not made of rock or oak. I am truly not made of rock!"
Before Socrates has emptied the cup the gaze of the viewer focuses on Phaedo. With tears streaming down his face, Phaedo, from his position against the wall, looks silently across at Socrates.

Then his face is transformed into that of the narrator Phaedo, who, as at the beginning, is sitting on the bench, gazing out into space.
Meanwhile it has become dark. Echecrates is standing in the deep shadow of a tree. He is only visible to the extent that light [from the moon or an invisible street lamp shines on him. Both remain silent and motionless for a while. Then Phaedo stands up and, shivering with cold, puts his jacket on.

ECHECRATES *whose face remains in the shadow*: How did it end? Did Socrates say anything else?

PHAEDO: When he had drunk the potion he walked up and down in the cell for a while, not saying a word. The poison began to have its effect. His legs began to feel heavy. He lay down on the bed. Naturally, the bailiff was there the whole time; that is the law. He pressed Socrates's legs from time to time and each time asked if he felt it. Socrates said: no. Finally he pulled his blanket over his face. But then he pushed it away again and asked for Crito. "Crito" – he was already speaking with difficulty – "we owe the offering of a cock to Asclepios. Make the offering. Don't forget!"

ECHECRATES: A thanks offering for recovery? What is that supposed to mean?

PHAEDO: Yes, we asked him that too. For recovery from "the illness of life" – perhaps.
Naturally, Crito said: Yes, yes, of course we will do that; but – perhaps there was something else he wanted to say? – But Socrates had covered his face again. He gave no further answers. In the meantime, the effect of the poison had reached his heart and his whole body began to convulse violently. Then, suddenly, he was calm. The bailiff pulled the blanket back and we saw that he was dead. Crito went to him immediately and closed his mouth and eyes. None of the rest of us could have done it.
Phaedo goes over to Echecrates, so that the face of each of them is now in darkness.
That is all I know. Thus died Socrates, our friend, the best of all men we had ever met – unsurpassed by anyone either in wisdom or in justice.

NOTES

1. See the first section of the *Phaedrus* dialogue [227a], in which Phaedrus recalls the advice which Acumenus, the father of Eryximachus, used to give.

2. Taken from the first scene of Aristophanes's *Frogs*, in which Dionysus, the god of theatre, goes down into the underworld to bring a real poet to Athens after the death of Aeschylus and Euripides: "The good ones are dead, and the living ones are bad" – and then he asks: "Where is Agathon?"

3. See the dialogue *Gorgias* [521a-522a].

4. This passage comes, in reality, from the *Phaedo* dialogue [115d].

5. See the *Symposium* 173d.

6. See *Phaedo* 62a 8.

7. See "Socrates's Speech in his defense" [20b].

8. These sentences are taken from the Judgment Myth, narrated at the end of *Gorgias*, and inserted here.

9. See *Gorgias* 527a.

10. This refers to the translation by Franz Boll which appeared in the Tusculum-Bücher series [Verlag E. Heimeran, München].

The plays published here were all recorded by German Television [Bayerischer Rundfunk]. The *Gorgias* dialogue was broadcast in March 1962 [repeated in November 1964]. The *Symposium* was broadcast in June 1965. Both plays were then broadcast by Austrian

Television. The director was Walter Rilla; the main performer was Heinz Moog [Burgtheater, Vienna]. – The *Death of Socrates* was planned for 1967.

In a slightly modified version all three plays were also broadcast as radio plays by Swiss Radio [Studio Bern] in the late autumn of 1966. [Director: Amido Hoffmann; main performer: Matthias Wieman].

NOTE: THE COUNTER ARGUMENTS

So many problems of a serious nature have been raised in relation to these works that it is difficult to know where to begin. However, the reason why I finally did not take them up can be expressed in one single sentence. My intention had been, in the current period, to lay before as many people as possible what was truly said and meant in the Platonic dialogues – not so much for the sake of historical record as for the sake of the living truth which has remained valid throughout the ages and which here, in an incomparable way, has taken concrete shape.

These "plays" do not expressly lay claim to literary value; rather they could be described as plays for teaching [Lehrstücke] – which still implies a significant standard, though one which it is not easy to formulate. However, some of the presuppositions and inevitable demands are clear.

It seems to me that the easiest question to answer is whether, generally speaking, it is at all feasible or even fitting to aim at making Plato's work accessible through use of "mass media." My answer is: teaching and learning are never possible unless the learners are sought out and reached precisely in the place they are – whether this place is congenial or not.

No one knew this better than Plato's Socrates, who never for a moment thought he was too important to speak about cobblers, weaver's shuttles, calves, and foals in order to communicate to the simplest folk what is meant by such difficult concepts as "idea" and "virtue." The greatness of this teacher consists in his knowing how to avoid any inadmissible simplification, which is the rock on which all attempts to teach and to pass on knowledge are liable to perish. And of course, the danger becomes all the more threatening the more sublime the subject matter and the coarser the methods used. But whether one is going to perish on this rock or not cannot be determined in advance. That can only be ascertained, as it were, on the spot.

That applies also to the most brutal demand, which almost made me capitulate. I am referring to the need for a radical abridgement of the text. Clearly, even with people who have a lively interest in learning, one cannot expect the average viewer to watch a program on Plato's work for longer than, say, an hour. Also, for better or for worse, one has to accept that a longer transmission time will not be granted. Besides, an American university colleague said to me, not without a touch of envy, that over there even that amount of time was not imaginable.

I would not have agreed to the required abridgement of the original if I had not been convinced that it is possible to capture the core of Plato's statement, and even – perhaps through abridgement – to make it have a stronger impact on the uninitiated. And even if the alternative question sometimes formulated by critics were to be properly posed, namely, what is the more desirable: to know nothing at all about Plato or, as in the present case, to be presented with such a minimal and approximate sense of the meaning? – even then I would say without hesitation that little is still better than nothing at all, assuming that the "sense" produced is accurate and perhaps even generates the desire for more precise knowledge.

The least problematic form of abridgement would seem to be the simple tightening of the text, which possibly makes the links in the chain of thought much clearer. The following comparison should show this; here, what I think is the best [German] translation[10] of a passage from the *Symposium* is juxtaposed with my own strongly abbreviated version of the text:

That should be enough about the beauty of the god, however much remains to be said; but now we have to speak about the virtue of Eros.	But Eros is not only beautiful, he is also good!
The most important point is that Eros does not suffer injustice, whether it is done by a god or to a god; or done by a human being or to a human being.	What does justice mean? That one is given what is his. But everyone serves Eros of his own free will – and so no injustice is done to anyone.
For he himself does not suffer through coercion when he suffers, since coercion cannot touch Eros; nor does he do what he does with coercion; for everyone serves Eros freely in everything. But what a person	

willingly allows to a willing person is declared by the rulers of the state – the laws – to be just.

But along with justice he has the greatest share of moderation. For there is agreement about the fact that this consists in the control of pleasures and desires. But there is no pleasure stronger than that of Eros; and if Eros controls his pleasures and desires he achieves a special level of moderation.

And with regard to courage even Ares cannot match Eros: for it is not Ares who possesses Eros but Eros who possesses Ares – the love for Aphrodite, as is said; but the one in possession is stronger than the possessed; and the one who controls the most courageous must be the most courageous of all.

So much for the justice, moderation and courage of the god; it only remains to speak of his wisdom. To the

What do self-control and moderation consist in? In controlling one's pleasures and desires. But Eros is stronger than all of them; he controls them all without exception.

And courage! Who was the victor in the fight between Ares and Eros? Not the god of war, but Eros!

Finally, as for justice – Eryximachus, you have spoken of your discipline, the art of healing; I must best of my ability I must now try not to be found wanting. And above all, to do my art proud as Eryximachus did his: the god is such a wise poet that he also makes others to be such, for everyone becomes a poet, "even someone who previously knew nothing about the muses," when Eros touches him. (Boll)

now speak of my art, poetry. Is it not Eros who makes someone into a poet? (Pieper)

Something much more difficult and questionable than abridgement by summarizing a passage of the text is, in our context, the unavoidable elimination of whole passages. Clearly, here we are faced with deciding what, in Plato's overall conception of things, is "essential" and what is not. It is only to be expected that an endless debate can be held about this without the prospect of ever arriving at a satisfactory conclusion. What I have done is to hold firmly to the fairly convincing and justifiable distinction which separates the "material" of a statement from the inner form which shapes it and which could be applied to a different kind of "material."

The "scientific" theories1of the time about the structure of the earth, for example, which in *Phaedo* Plato links with his description of the eschatological myth, are, I am convinced, part of the description of the shell in which – in Plato's own view – everything essential is housed. They are no more of the essence than, for example, the description of the field where judgment takes place at a crossroads in the underworld – which in no way means that

Plato did not take the cosmology of his day seriously and that it did not also play a part in determining his notions about the world beyond. However, this "material" can be surrendered without one iota being lost from the core of Plato's statement, which in this case says, above all: the ultimate manifestation of the true result of our existence in this life takes place on the other side of death, in an event which is beyond the compass of our imagination and which, in symbolic, mythical speech is called "Judgment of the Dead."

One final point: it is obvious that a text of Plato simplified in this way by omissions and by the highlighting of the essential aspects cannot be left without some kind of commentary. The technical problem resulting from this was that text and commentary needed to be, in the mind of the viewer, distinguishable from one another. In each of the three plays I have tried to achieve this in a different way. In *Gorgias* the commentary is done through use of the modern technique of a framing dialogue into which Plato's texts are inserted. In the *Symposium*, which has the least need of extensive explanation, the task is left to a speaker who remains invisible. In the last play, on the other hand, the commentary is woven into the report in which Phaedo, himself a figure of Plato's appearing in the dialogue, narrates to a visitor the events of Socrates's last days.

All of these efforts are aimed solely at awakening in the spectator some fundamental certainties about our existence – underpinning them and bringing them to life in his consciousness: the certainty, for instance, that the main point of human speech does not lie in the intentional influencing of another person but in the imparting of truth, that is, in shared communication about reality; that committing an injustice is infinitely worse than suffering one; that in a deeply erotic experience man is given a promise that is not to be fulfilled in this life; that our soul possesses indestructible being; that it will be judged on the other side of death; and that unending participation in the life of God awaits the person who wants good.

On the other hand, anyone who – no matter how scholarly the manner in which he studies the original text – is more concerned with Socrates than with truth and does not see that insights of this kind are not what is really meant, and does not take possession of them anew: such a person has, despite everything, failed to see what we are really being offered in Plato's work.

FROM THE BLURB of the Kösel German edition

These "Platonic" plays are not just convenient short versions for readers under time pressure. It is true that a resolute attempt has been made to give the modern person, the non-specialist, new access to Plato's work which has been able to keep philosophical discussion on tenterhooks right down to the present day. However, anyone who treads this path, here freed of rubble, and approaches the much acclaimed works *Gorgias, Symposium, Phaedo,* is not to expect any inadmissible simplifications. Instead he can expect to encounter the dialectical explosiveness found in the original text, with nothing watered down. And what has happened many times with television audiences may also happen to the reader: that the irresistible urge arises to become acquainted with the exact words of the Platonic dialogues – the others as well – in an unabridged and direct form.